Hamid,

With deep appreciation for your unwavering support & friendship.

Charles . 9/1/2016

Alphanomics:
The Informational
Underpinnings of Market
Efficiency

Alphanomics: The Informational Underpinnings of Market Efficiency

Charles M. C. Lee
Stanford University, USA
clee8@stanford.edu

Eric C. So
Massachusetts Institute of Technology, USA
eso@mit.edu

the essence of knowledge
Boston — Delft

Foundations and Trends® in Accounting

Published, sold and distributed by:
now Publishers Inc.
PO Box 1024
Hanover, MA 02339
United States
Tel. +1-781-985-4510
www.nowpublishers.com
sales@nowpublishers.com

Outside North America:
now Publishers Inc.
PO Box 179
2600 AD Delft
The Netherlands
Tel. +31-6-51115274

The preferred citation for this publication is

C. M. C. Lee and E. C. So. *Alphanomics: The Informational Underpinnings of Market Efficiency.* Foundations and Trends® in Accounting, vol. 9, nos. 2–3, pp. 59–258, 2014.

This Foundations and Trends® issue was typeset in LaTeX using a class file designed by Neal Parikh. Printed on acid-free paper.

ISBN: 978-1-60198-892-8
© 2015 C. M. C. Lee and E. C. So

Foundations and Trends® in Accounting
Volume 9, Issue 2–3, 2014
Editorial Board

Editorial Scope

Topics

Foundations and Trends® in Accounting publishes survey and tutorial articles in the following topics:

- Auditing
- Corporate governance
- Cost management
- Disclosure
- Event studies/Market efficiency studies
- Executive compensation
- Financial reporting
- Financial statement analysis and equity valuation
- Management control
- Performance measurement
- Taxation

Information for Librarians

Foundations and Trends® in Accounting, 2014, Volume 9, 4 issues. ISSN paper version 1554-0642. ISSN online version 1554-0650. Also available as a combined paper and online subscription.

Foundations and Trends® in Accounting
Vol. 9, Nos. 2–3 (2014) 59–258
© 2015 C. M. C. Lee and E. C. So
DOI: 10.1561/1400000022

the essence of knowledge

Alphanomics: The Informational Underpinnings of Market Efficiency

Charles M. C. Lee
Stanford University, USA
clee8@stanford.edu

Eric C. So
Massachusetts Institute of Technology, USA
eso@mit.edu

Contents

Abstract

This monograph is a compact introduction to empirical research on market efficiency, behavioral finance, and fundamental analysis. The first section reviews the evolution of academic thinking on market efficiency. Section 2 introduces the noise trader model as an alternative framework for market-related research. Section 3 surveys the growing literature on the causes and consequences of investor sentiment. Section 4 examines the role of fundamental analysis in value investing. Section 5 contains a survey of the literature on arbitrage costs and constraints, and Section 6 discusses research methodology issues associated with the need to distinguish between mispricing from risk.

C. M. C. Lee and E. C. So. *Alphanomics: The Informational Underpinnings of Market Efficiency*. Foundations and Trends® in Accounting, vol. 9, nos. 2–3, pp. 59–258, 2014. Copyright © 2015.
DOI: 10.1561/1400000022.

Foreword

Assumptions matter. They confine the flexibility that we believe is available to us as researchers, and they define the topics we deem worthy of study. Perhaps more insidiously, once we've lived with them long enough, they can disappear entirely from our consciousness.

Mainstream accounting and economic thought is shaped by classical information economics — the study of normative behavior under full rationality assumptions. While this powerful paradigm has proved highly instructive, it has also engendered an unfortunate tendency for economists to attribute unlimited processing ability to decision makers. We view this tendency as unfortunate, because it can inhibit the development of other potentially promising avenues of research.

In the area of market-based research, the assumption of unbounded rationality has produced a deep-seated faith in market efficiency that, for many years, detracted from potentially fruitful inquiries along alternative paths. As economists, we tend to take for granted the efficacy of the arbitrage mechanism, generally assuming that it involves few constraints, and little cost or risk. Faith in the arbitrage mechanism has stunted the development of research in mainstream economics on the dynamic process of information acquisition, analysis, and aggregation. Market prices are often presumed to be correct, as if by fiat, and the process by which they become correct is trivialized.

3

The depth of our collective faith in market efficiency is evident from our course offerings. At most top business schools today, investment classes are taught by financial economists trained in equilibrium thinking. In these classes, the efficient market hypothesis (EMH) is typically offered as the intellectual high ground — an inevitable outcome of rational thinking. Students are taught that market-clearing conditions require prices to reflect all currently available information. This line of reasoning persists, despite the fact that it conforms neither to logic nor to evidence.

This research monograph is intended to be a compact introduction to academic research on market efficiency, behavioral finance, and fundamental analysis. In the first two sections, we review the evolution of academic thinking on market efficiency, and introduce the noise trader model as a rational alternative. In the next four sections, we expand on several concepts introduced in the first two sections. Specifically, in Section 3, we survey the literature on investor sentiment and its role as a source of both risks and returns. In Section 4, we discuss the role of fundamental analysis in value investing. In Section 5, we survey the literature on limits to arbitrage, and in Section 6, we discuss research methodology issues associated with the need to distinguish mispricing from risk.

Some of the questions we will address include: Why do we believe markets are efficient? What problems have this belief engendered? What factors can impede and/or facilitate market efficiency? What roles do investor sentiment and costly arbitrage play in determining an equilibrium level of informational efficiency? What is the essence of value investing? How is it related to fundamental analysis (the study of historical financial data)? And how might we distinguish between risk and mispricing-based explanations for predictability patterns in returns?

The degree to which markets are efficient affects the demand for accounting research in investment decisions, regulatory standard-setting decisions, performance evaluations, corporate governance, contract design, executive compensation, and corporate disclosure decisions. One's belief about market efficiency also dictates our research design, and in particular the role played by market prices in the analysis. Perhaps most importantly, given the intended audience of this volume, one's view about market efficiency will have a profound effect on the shape of one's research agenda. In fact, what a researcher chooses to study in the capital market area is, we believe, largely a function of her level of faith in the informational efficiency of these markets.

It has been 35 years since Michael Jensen famously proclaimed at a *Journal of Financial Economics* (JFE) symposium: "I believe there is no other proposition in economics which has more solid empirical evidence supporting it than the Efficient Market Hypothesis." [Jensen, 1978, p. 95]. Less often quoted, but perhaps even more on the mark, were Jensen's remarks at the end of the same article. Commenting on the evidence presented at the symposium about market-pricing anomalies, he wrote: "I have little doubt that in the next several years we will document further anomalies and begin to sort out and understand their causes. The result will not be abandonment of the 'efficiency' concept, nor of asset-pricing models. Five years from now, however, we will, as a profession, have a much better understanding of these concepts than we now possess, and we will have a much more fundamental understanding of the world around us." This monograph is an attempt to summarize what we have learned since, and what we as a profession have to look forward to in the future.

The 2013 Nobel Memorial Prize in Economics was shared by three Americans — Eugene Fama, Lars Peter Hansen, and Robert Shiller. For many of us who have followed the EMH debate over the years, the decision to honor Fama and Shiller together is not without irony, given the radical differences in their views on the subject. Fama was honored for his work in the 1960s showing that market prices are accurate reflections of available information. Shiller is honored largely for circumscribing that theory in the 1980s by showing that prices can deviate from rationality. In awarding them the prize, the Royal Swedish Academy of Sciences notes that collectively the three professors' work "laid the foundation for the current understanding of asset prices." In characterizing this contribution, the committee said their findings "showed that markets were moved by a mix of rational calculus and human behavior."

Markets are moved by a mix of rational calculus and human behavior. We have certainly come a long way since the days of the 1978 JFE symposium! As Jensen predicted, financial economists have not abandoned rational calculus or the concept of 'efficiency.' The power of equilibrium thinking is alive and well. At the same time, 35 years later, we have also come to acknowledge the importance of human behavior and arbitrage costs in asset-pricing. As a profession, many more of us are now willing to entertain, and wrestle with, the limitations and problems of an imperfect market. In this sense, we have indeed come to a much better place in terms of our understanding of the world around us.

In recent decades, the focus of academic research on market efficiency has gradually shifted from the general to the more specific. While earlier studies tended to view the matter as a yes/no debate, most recent studies now acknowledge the impossibility of fully efficient markets, and have focused instead on factors that could materially affect the timely incorporation of information. An extensive literature in finance has developed that examine the effect of "noise trader demand", or "investor sentiment" (broadly defined as price pressures of a non-fundamental origin). There is now substantial evidence that investor sentiment can affect asset-pricing, as well as real economic decisions, such as corporate finance, investments, dividend policies, and disclosure decisions. At the same time, increasing attention is being paid to how regulatory decisions could either impede or enhance market efficiency through their effect on information arbitrageurs.

Whatever one's view is of market efficiency, few scholars today deny the fact that active asset management, with "beating the market" as its central mandate, is today a large and thriving business. The reason our financial markets are even remotely efficient is because sufficient resources are being spent each day on keeping it so.[1] The agents who acquire and process new information aspire to make a profit from their

---

[1] As discussed in more detail in Section 1, we estimate the amount of asset-under-management (AUM) controlled by professional *active* managers across asset classes to be at least $60 trillion USD as of the end of 2012. The U.S. mutual fund market alone exceeds $6 trillion, and the hedge fund market is at least $2 trillion (See the 2013 Investment Company Factbook, available at http://www.icifactbook.org/).

investment. Their continued survival speaks powerfully to magnitude of the aggregate mispricing in equilibrium. At the same time, these purveyors of information face a complex production function, with multiple costs and risks, including: time-varying capital constraints, moral hazard problems, risk management issues, security lending costs, and various practical implementation challenges. Market efficiency is inevitably a function of the cost constraints faced by information arbitrageurs.[2]

In our view, a naïve form of efficiency, in which market prices are assumed to equal fundamental value, is a grossly inadequate starting point for much of today's market-related research.[3] To us, this is an oversimplification that underweights the role of costly information and fails to capture the richness of market-pricing dynamics and the process of price discovery. Prices do not adjust to fundamental value instantly by fiat. In reality market prices are buffeted by a continuous flow of information, or rumors and innuendos disguised as information. Individuals reacting to these signals, or pseudo-signals, cannot easily calibrate the extent to which their own signal is already reflected in price. This noisy process of price discovery requires time and takes effort, and is only achieved at substantial cost to society.

When information processing is costly, research opportunities abound. Given noisy prices and costly arbitrage, academic research can add value by improving the cost-effectiveness of the arbitrage mechanism. Some of this research will lead to superior techniques for identifying arbitrage opportunities. Other research will focus on sources of systematic noise, exploring behavioral and non-fundamental reasons why prices might diverge from value. Still others, such as work on earnings quality or fundamental analysis, will help to narrow the plausibility bounds around the value estimates of traded securities.

Thus it clearly takes a great deal of capital and resources to attain the level of pricing efficiency we currently enjoy.

[2]We define arbitrage as information trading aimed at exploiting market imperfections. As discussed later, this definition is broader than the definition found in some finance textbooks.

[3]Throughout this discourse, fundamental value is defined as the expected value of future dividends, conditional on currently available information. See Section 1 for a more detailed definition of the efficient market hypothesis (EMH).

Finally, research into arbitrage constraints and market design issues can help us to better understand and manage the costs faced by those who seek to acquire information and make markets more efficient. How might the incentives of these agents be affected by changes in security market regulations and mandatory corporate disclosure rules (such as fair value accounting or the adoption of IFRS)? How is the information acquisition and alpha extraction process being impacted by Big Data? To us, a wide world of research opportunities opens up once we are willing to lift the hood, and peer behind the assumption of market efficiency.

Much of this research has a utilitarian focus. It is decision driven, interdisciplinary, and prospective in nature. It assumes a user, rather than a preparer, orientation toward accounting information. It does not assume that the market price is equivalent to fundamental value. Rather, it produces independent estimates of firm value that may be used to challenge, and perhaps discipline, prices. Its end goal is to improve the allocation of scarce resources through more cost-effective usage of information in solving significant problems in financial economics.

This monograph is dedicated to the kind of decision-driven and prospectively-focused research that is much needed in a market constantly seeking to become *more* efficient. We refer to this type of research as "Alphanomics", the informational economics behind market efficiency. The "Alpha" portion refers to the abnormal returns, or financial rewards, which provide the incentive for some subpopulation of investors to engage in information acquisition and costly arbitrage activities. The "Nomics" refers to the economics of alpha extraction, which encompasses the costs and incentives of informational arbitrage as a sustainable business proposition.

We caution the reader on two caveats. First, the evidence we survey here focuses primarily on publicly traded equity securities. We acknowledge that in finance, an extensive literature explores related topics across multiple asset classes in a more global setting. Although we cover this literature only tangentially, many of the same principles discussed here apply across other asset classes. Second, we are focused on market efficiency in an informational sense — that is, whether and how prices incorporate available information. Tobin [1984] entertains a broader definition of economic efficiency that we find intriguing, particularly his views on the "functional efficiency" of free markets. For parsimony, our monograph does not tread in that direction, but interested readers are encouraged to include Professor Tobin's work in their list of must-read references.

This work is made up of six sections. The first two sections draw heavily from the writings of financial economists. In Section 1, titled "The Magic of Markets," we revisit the theoretical foundations of the EMH, and discuss some of the limitations and biases it engenders. Some have compared the EMH to "Newtonian physics" in the sense that while we know it does not hold precisely, the theory is a safe operating assumption for practical purposes. We critically evaluate this claim, and discuss situations where the EMH falls particularly short.

Section 2 introduces a simple *Noise Trader Model* ("NTM") first featured in Shiller [1984]. A particularly appealing aspect of the NTM is its explicit recognition of the role played by information costs. In contrast to the EMH, which assumes information costs are trivial, the role for information arises endogenously in the NTM and the cost of information acquisition and analysis has direct implications for equilibrium pricing.

Section 3 expands the discussion of *Investor Sentiment*. In this section, we survey the extensive literature on noise trading and investor sentiment that has developed over the past three decades. We show that evidence in favor of a role for human behavior and investor sentiment in asset-pricing is now extensive. We also discuss the implications of these findings for the future of accounting research.

Section 4 examines *Equity Valuation*. An independent estimate of firm value is needed if information arbitrageurs are to challenge and discipline price. We discuss the role of historical accounting information in the formulation of such an estimate. Using the residual income model (RIM) as a framework, we integrate the investment approaches advocated by such legendary investors as: Ben Graham, Warren Buffett, and Joel Greenblatt. This analysis shows that the strategies espoused by these investors actually dovetail nicely with the recent evidence from academic research on the predictability of stock returns.

Section 5 examines *Limits to Arbitrage*. In the NTM, the extent to which prices may wander away from fundamentals is a function of the costs faced by informed arbitrageurs. Thus reducing arbitrage costs will lead directly to greater pricing efficiency. We dissect the major components of these costs and discuss how each component might impact common investment strategies employed by hedge funds. We also discuss academic studies that shed light on the cost constraints faced by arbitrageurs.

Section 6 focuses on *Research Methodology*. In this section, we review research design issues for academics interested in working on questions related to market efficiency. Specifically, we discuss techniques for distinguishing between whether a predictable pattern in prices is due to risk or mispricing. We also speculate on future research directions in this area, using recent studies as illustrations.

In sum, this monograph presents and promotes a more nuanced view of market efficiency. It may be viewed as our attempt to reconcile the *theory* of market efficiency, so popular among academics, with the *practice* of active investing, so prevalent in industry. Active investing is big business, and it is rooted in the basic premise that the search for information not yet reflected in prices can be a worthy pursuit. It is difficult to begin serious academic analyses of this industry without an economic framework that accommodates, and even anticipates, the continued existence of mispricing in equilibrium. We offer such a framework.

1

The Magic of Markets

In this section, we trace the progression of economic thought on market efficiency.[1] We discuss what is meant by the efficient market hypothesis (EMH), and some of the most pressing problems that have resulted from the profession's undue reliance on market efficiency. Beginning with Hayek [1945], we review the informational role of markets in free enterprise systems. We then discuss the untenable case for perfectly efficient markets [Grossman and Stiglitz, 1980] and argue for a broader research agenda that recognizes the importance of the market for information.

1.1 The value of markets in society

In his justly famous treatise on the subject of knowledge aggregation in society, Hayek [1945] contrasted centralized-planning with a market-based economy based on decentralized decision making. Hayek noted that economic planning involves two types of knowledge: (1) scientific knowledge (knowledge about theoretical or technical principles

---

[1]For other survey studies that cover overlapping themes, see Lee [2001], Richardson et al. [2010], Asness and Liew [2014], and Campbell [2014].

and rules), and (2) specific knowledge (knowledge of particular circumstances of time and place). Recognizing that even the best central planner does not have adequate access to knowledge of the second
type, Hayek argued that market-based economies in which resource
allocation decisions are decentralized will always dominate centralized
planning. This is because in a rational economic order, efficient social
planning will always depend on "the utilization of knowledge not given
to anyone in its entirety" (p. 520).

With the benefit of hindsight, the genius of Hayek is clear. After
WWII, multiple country-level, paired-experiments emerged that offered
a remarkable glimpse into the power of market-based planning: North
and South Korea; East and West Germany; Taiwan and Communist
China. In each case, holding constant cultural and genetic factors,
decentralized economies dominated centrally-planned ones. This domi-
nance is seen not merely in terms of personal economic wealth (that is,
per capita GDP). On almost every conceivable metric of social wellness
(education; opportunity; nutrition and healthcare; life expectancy; and
basic human needs), the market-based systems dominated.[2] As Mar-
garet Thatcher, champion of the free market gospel, once quipped:
"capitalism *is* humanitarianism." In short, markets work and there is
little wonder that the 20th century has been called "the Hayek Century" [Cassidy, 2000].

But what then gives the market-based economies their magic? It
boils down to better resource allocation through decentralized decision
making. As Hayek observed, the essential planning problem of society
involves rapid adaptation to changing circumstances. It is an information game that the central planner cannot hope to win. It follows
then that "the man (woman) on the spot" is the best person to make
resource allocation decisions.[3]

---

[2]A good resource for those interested in broad measures of social progress is:
www.socialprogressimperative.org.

[3]Hayek argued that due to this information game, planning must be decentralized. Government intervention in a free market only serves to forestall economic ail-
ments and could lead to political oppression. In the *Road to Serfdom*, Hayek [1944]
warns ominously: "the unforeseen but inevitable consequences of socialist planning
create a state of affairs in which, if the policy is to be pursued, totalitarian forces
will get the upper hand."

And what role do *prices* play in all this? Consider what the "man (woman) on the spot" needs to make resource allocation decisions. At a minimum, she needs to know the relative scarcity of things — the value of the inputs and outputs relevant to her decision. This information is quickly and succinctly summarized by prices. The pricing system is a vital knowledge aggregation mechanism in free markets. To the extent that market prices are meaningful indicators of relative scarcity, they help facilitate decentralized planning. Price, in short, is a *public good* that is essential in enabling decentralized decision making.

Given these basic tenets of free market economics, the efficiency with which market prices assimilate new information assumes an importance beyond academic debates over the size of the abnormal returns earned by hedge fund managers. If asset prices drive decentralized decisions and decentralized decision making drives free enterprise systems, then prices play a key informational role in free market economies. This is because such economies depend on their markets to set prices, which in turn determine resource allocation throughout the system.

We thus draw two key lessons from Hayek: (1) the informational role of markets in knowledge aggregation is of great value to society, and (2) asset prices that reflect the value of goods (and services) are central to the development of free market systems.

Notice, however, that neither Hayek , nor the broader Austrian school of economics to which he belonged, was focused on the specifics of *how* markets become efficient, or *when* the knowledge aggregation process might fail. These earlier works were focused on the central battle of their day: whether market systems are better than centrally planned ones. They are largely silent with respect to the economics of information acquisition and analysis, and the factors that might cause markets to become more or less price efficient. These issues were not their primary concern.

The idea that markets serve as powerful aggregators of knowledge, first proposed by Hayek, has in our day morphed into what we refer to as the EMH. In the next subsection we discuss why this turn of events has led to some inevitable problems.

1.2   The joint equilibrium problem

Some economists today believe the EMH is the "moral high ground", arguing that the existence of mispricing necessarily implies off-equilibrium (thus non-economic) thinking. In fact, the exact opposite is true. In terms of equilibrium thinking, it is the simplistic and naïve form of EMH that is conceptually flawed and intellectually untenable.

Statements regarding the efficiency of market prices must first recognize the existence of two interrelated but distinct markets. First, there is the market for the assets themselves — what people will pay for fractional ownership of various assets. In addition, if it is costly to evaluate asset and assign fair values, there will exist another market on information about these assets. Participants in this second market buy and sell information about the underlying assets. These participants incur costs to 'buy' (that is, acquire) information with the expectation that they can 'sell' (that is, profit) from this information, either through trading (in the case of investors) or other means (for example, sell-side analysts). A more complete view of equilibrium requires both markets to clear. In other words, supply must equal demand in *both* the asset market, and the market for information about these assets.

In discussing the impossibility of perfectly efficient markets, Grossman and Stiglitz make the following observation:

> *We have argued that because information is costly, prices cannot perfectly reflect the information which is available, since if it did, those who spend resources to obtain it would receive no compensation. There is a fundamental conflict between the efficiency with which markets spread information and the incentives to acquire information.* Grossman and Stiglitz [1980, p. 405]

Their point is simple. When information costs are non-trivial, some amount of mispricing must remain in equilibrium. This must be the case if informed traders are to be sufficiently compensated. In other words, market clearing conditions in this joint equilibrium (when supply equals demand in both markets) require asset prices to bear the marks of inefficiency.

Given the inextricable link between these two markets, focusing on either in isolation would be foolhardy. If we focus solely on the asset market, for example, we will observe "pricing anomalies", whose roots lie in the market for information. These asset-pricing aberrations can only be understood in the context of supply and demand in the parallel market for information. Larger mispricings will remain, for example, when the cost of acquiring and exploiting information about a firm is higher. This might be the case if the company's operations are more complex, its accounting is more opaque, or if informational extraction costs, such as market liquidity, and short-selling costs (that is, the costs of profitably exploiting value-relevant information) are higher.[4]

A central problem with the EMH is the assumption that the costs associated with informational arbitrage are trivial or unimportant. Both theory and evidence suggest that financial economists need to pay more attention to the costs and incentives in the market for information. The reason *most* individuals in society can rely on market prices to make their everyday decisions is because *some* individuals in society do not. While it might be alright for most (even the vast majority of) individuals in society to assume "the price is right" — that is, to free ride on the efforts of information arbitrageurs — economists who study how markets operates should not be counted among them.

Most people can assume a car will run each time the key is turned, however their auto mechanics cannot afford to do so. In fact, auto mechanics remain in business precisely because cars do not always operate as intended. Likewise financial economists interested in the informational role of markets need to understand how the market for information operates, and how frictions in that market can lead to pricing anomalies in the asset market. They need to look under the hood. It would be an abdication of responsibility for them not to.

---

[4]Blocher et al. [2013] provide an excellent example of the joint equilibrium problem in the context of short-selling constraints. Empirically, Beneish et al. [2015] link this phenomenon to nine well-known pricing anomalies in the equity market.

1.3   What do we mean by market efficiency?

Stripped down to its core, the efficient market hypothesis (EMH) is the simple proposition that market prices incorporate all available information. The original EMH literature is careful to condition this statement on a particular set of available information (see, for example, Fama [1965, 1970, 1991]). Different forms of the EMH (strong, semi-strong, and weak) are then defined in terms of the rapidity and accuracy of price adjustment to news, conditional on different information sets. Early applications of the EMH in accounting also acknowledged that the speed and accuracy of price adjustment to new information is a continuous process, and does not occur instantaneously (see, for example, Dyckman and Morse [1986, p. 2]).

Most empirical tests of market efficiency have focused on the predictability of returns. The idea is that if current market prices incorporate all available information, then future returns should be largely unpredictable. Or, at least any patterns of predictability that we observe in future returns should not be easily exploited after transaction costs. This version of the EMH is often evoked, for example, in deriving equilibrium conditions in asset-pricing models. It has been variously referred to as the "competitively efficient markets" hypothesis [Rubinstein, 2001], or the "no arbitrage condition". An even more descriptive moniker, we think, is the "No Free Lunch" assumption. Markets that are in equilibrium should rarely, if ever, offer a free lunch.

Tests of the "no free lunch" hypothesis run quickly into a serious challenge, which Fama [1970, 1991] famously refers to as the "joint hypothesis problem".[5] To make any statement about market efficiency, we need to assert how the market *should* reflect information — in other words, we need an equilibrium asset-pricing model. For example, the Capital Asset Pricing Model (CAPM) states that the expected return on any security is proportional to the risk of that security as measured by its sensitivity to market returns, referred to as 'Beta', and

---

[5]See Asness and Liew [2014] for a good discussion of the work by Fama and Shiller from the perspective of former academics who are now active fund managers. Campbell [2014] provides a more academic review of their work.

nothing else should matter. Suppose we find evidence against the predictive power of Beta for cross-sectional returns. One possibility is the EMH holds, but CAPM is a poor model of how investors set prices. Perhaps prices do reflect all information, but there are other risk factors besides market returns that investors are being compensated for bearing. Another possibility is that the CAPM is in fact how investors *should* set prices, but they are failing at it because of some sort of behavioral error or bias. Yet a third possibility is that the EMH and the CAPM are both wrong. It is difficult to sort out where the problem lies.

It has been argued that the joint hypothesis problem renders the EMH impossible to conclusively reject [Fama, 1970, 1991]. Indeed, this problem does limit what researchers can say about market efficiency on the basis of return predictability alone. However, there are now multiple methods for evaluating the reasonableness of a claim about market mispricing besides returns prediction. Some of these involve examining ancillary evidence about firms' future cash flows, operating profits, short-window earnings announcement returns, analyst forecast revisions, probability of distress or delisting, or short-sale activities, etc. Other studies [for example, Daniel and Titman, 1997, Hirshleifer et al., 2012, Ohlson and Bilinski, 2015] rely on common sense "reasonableness" tests to distinguish mispricing-based from risk-based explanations for returns predictability. The main point being as researchers, we now have at our disposal a large set of holistic, "weight of evidence," approaches that can help us to discriminate between risk and mispricing (this is the main subject of Section 6; we also touch on it in this section, in Section 1.7.3).[6]

As difficult as it might be to disprove the "No Free Lunch" hypothesis, this version of the EMH is not the main problem. As capital market research has evolved over time, a much stronger and more insidious form of the EMH has gained currency. It is what we refer to as the "Price is Right" hypothesis. Applied to equity markets, this view of market efficiency asserts that a company's stock price is an

---

[6]Also see Richardson et al. [2010] for a discussion of non-price-based tests that can help discriminate between risk and mispricing-based explanations for returns predictability.

optimal forecast of the present value of its expected future dividends ($P_t = V_t, \forall t$). Notationally, this view is often expressed in the following form:

$$P_t = V_t \equiv \sum_{i=1}^{\infty} \frac{E_t(D_{t+i})}{(1+r)^i}, \tag{1.1}$$

where V_t is defined as the stock's fundamental value at time t, $E_t(D_{t+i})$ is the expected future dividend for period $t + i$ based on information available at time t, and r is the appropriate risk-adjusted discount rate for the expected dividend stream. Equation (1) asserts that P_t, the stock price at time t, is equivalent to the expected value of future dividends, V_t.

Over time, the Price is Right view of markets has acquired the status of an operating assumption among many researchers. For example, in the information content literature in accounting (including both short-window event studies and long-window association studies), price is commonly interpreted as a de facto proxy for the expected value of future dividends, and stock returns are deemed to reflect changes in the present value of expected future dividends. In the extensive value-relevance literature [Holthausen and Watts, 2001, Barth et al., 2001], price is deemed to be a normative benchmark for firm value. The assumption that price is equivalent to the present value of expected future dividends appears more explicitly in valuation studies, typically as the first assumption in the paper (see, for example, Feltham and Ohlson [1999], Zhang [2000], and Dechow et al. [1999]).

In finance, this assumption has become a cornerstone of empirical asset-pricing, particularly when interpreting realized returns. For example, highly influential work by Campbell [1991] and Vuolteenaho [2002] decomposes realized returns under the assumption that movements in stock prices mirror movements in V_t. In a zero-sum attribution exercise where price equals value, what is not attributable to cash flows is, of necessity, attributed to discount rates. Thus, due to an uncritical application of the EMH, the unexplained volatility in stock prices is now widely interpreted in the empirical asset-pricing literature as evidence of time-varying expected returns.[7]

---

[7]Some may argue that Equation (1) is itself too naïve, as it does not allow for time-varying expected returns. In our view, this argument is a red herring. Of course,

The problem is that "No Free Lunch" does not imply "The Price is Right". In his seminal study on the role of mass psychology in markets, Shiller made the following observation:

> Returns on speculative assets are nearly unforecastable; this fact is the basis of the most important argument in the oral tradition against a role for mass psychology in speculative markets. One form of this argument claims that because real returns are nearly unforecastable, the real prices of stocks is close to the intrinsic value, that is, the present value with constant discount rate of optimally forecasted future real dividends. *This argument for the efficient market hypothesis represents one of the most remarkable errors in the history of economic thought. It is remarkable in the immediacy of its logical error and in the sweep and implications of its conclusion.* [Shiller, 1984, pp. 458–459] (emphasis is ours).

With a little thought, Shiller's point becomes obvious. If price is equal to value at all times, then indeed returns will be unforecastable. In other words, if the price is always right ("A"), then there will indeed be no free lunch ("B"). However, the reverse does not follow — it is possible for prices to vary far from fundamental values without presenting any easy money (that is, although "A" implies "B"; "B" does not imply "A").[8]

Equation (1) is predicated on the fact that we can derive an ex ante estimate of the cost-of-capital (risk-adjusted) appropriate for a firm's risk level. It would make no sense otherwise. However, irrespective of how a firm's expected return varies over time, at any given point in time one should be able to provide a point estimate for its expected return (a constant equivalent discount rate for its expected cash flows) based on currently available information. Our point is that given *any* reasonable estimate of r, Price should not be viewed as equivalent to Value. We discuss related issues in more detail later. Specifically, in Section 1.7.2, we cover the evidence on the excessive volatility of market-wide stock prices. In Section 5, we examine how funding constraints on arbitrage capital could give rise to time-variation in expected returns. Finally in Section 6, we revisit the issue of time-varying expected returns as an explanation for cross-sectional stock market anomalies.

[8]Consider the simple example where Price = Value + ε, and ε follows a random walk, or long-term mean reverting process. If the investment horizon of the typical arbitrageur is longer than the time it takes for ε to make significant progress toward zero, then arbitrageurs will not be able to profit from the mispricing.

The relevant point for capital market research is that just because returns are difficult to forecast, we should not jump to the conclusion that price is equal to intrinsic value. As we discuss below, much of the mess we find ourselves in today in empirical asset-pricing comes from a failure to heed Shiller's warning. But first, let's revisit the root arguments for market efficiency.

1.4   The conceptual case for efficiency

The traditional defense for market efficiency boils down to a visceral faith in the mechanism of arbitrage.[9] Most economists who believe markets are efficient view it as an inevitable outcome of continuous arbitrage. If a particular piece of value-relevant information is not incorporated into price, there will be powerful economic incentives to uncover it, and to trade on it. As a result of these arbitrage forces, price will adjust to fully reflect the information. Individual agents within the economy may behave irrationally, but we expect arbitrage forces to keep prices in line. Faith in the efficacy of this mechanism is a cornerstone of modern financial economics.

In fact, moving from the mechanics of arbitrage to the efficient market hypothesis involves an enormous leap of faith. It is akin to believing that the ocean is flat, simply because we have observed the forces of gravity at work on a glass of water. No one questions the effect of gravity, or the fact that water is always seeking its own level. But it is a stretch to infer from this observation that oceans should look like millponds on a still summer night. If oceans were flat, how do we explain predictable patterns, such as tides and currents? How can we account for the existence of waves, and of surfers? More to the point, if

---

[9]Some finance textbooks define arbitrage as "the simultaneous purchase and sale of the same, or essentially similar, security in two different markets for advantageously different prices" (see, for example, Sharpe and Alexander [1990]). This definition is too narrow for our purposes, because it implies an undertaking that requires no capital and entails no risk. In reality, almost all arbitrage requires capital, and is risky. Therefore, throughout this discourse, we will define arbitrage as information trading aimed at profiting from imperfections in the current price. Under this definition, arbitrage is based on costly information, and typically involves some risk.

we are in the business of training surfers, does it make sense to begin by assuming that waves, in theory, do not exist?

A more measured, and more descriptive, statement is that the ocean is constantly trying to become flat. In reality, market prices are buffeted by a continuous flow of information, or rumors and innuendos disguised as information. Individuals reacting to these signals, or pseudo-signals,[10] cannot fully calibrate the extent to which their own signal is already reflected in price. Prices move as they trade on the basis of their imperfect informational endowments. Eventually, through trial and error, the aggregation process is completed and prices adjust to fully reveal the impact of a particular signal. But by that time, many new signals have arrived, causing new turbulence. As a result, the ocean is in a constant state of restlessness. The market is in a continuous state of adjustment.

In this analogy, market efficiency is a journey, not a destination. Therefore, the pertinent questions about market efficiency are not yes or no, because strictly speaking the answer is always no. Price discovery is an on-going process and the current price of a security is best regarded as a noisy and incomplete proxy for a security's true fundamental value. In this context, the research focus should be on deriving an independent measure of fundamental value, and on understanding the dynamics of market price discovery. Rather than assume market efficiency, our research efforts are better focused on how, when, and why prices adjust (or fail to adjust) to information.

1.5 Can mispricing exist in equilibrium?

The descriptive validity of the above analogy depends on the continued existence of mispricings. Is it possible for mispricing to exist in equilibrium? Certainly. In fact, it strikes us as self-evident that arbitrage cannot exist without *some* amount of mispricing. Arbitrageurs are creatures of the very gap created by mispricing. Therefore, either both mispricing and arbitrage exist in equilibrium, or neither will. If by

---

[10]Pseudo signals have the appearance, but not the substance, of news. Trading on the basis of pseudo signals is one source noise trading, as described by Black [1986].

some mystical force, prices always adjust instantly to the right value, we would have no arbitrageurs. Therefore, if we believe that arbitrage is an equilibrium phenomenon, we must necessarily believe that *some* amount of mispricing is also an equilibrium phenomenon.

It may be useful to frame this discussion in terms of Hayek [1945]. Hayek addresses the vital role of markets in aggregating information across heterogeneously informed traders, but his work does not focus on the incentives for information acquisition and arbitrage. We argue that in order for the price discovery process featured in Hayek [1945] to operate effectively, sufficient incentives must exist in equilibrium to incentivize the information acquirers. In effect, the very reliability of prices depends on a sufficient level of mispricing to ensure that arbitrage continues to function. Because sustained arbitrage depends on the continued existence of exploitable opportunities, a free and competitive market is almost necessarily inefficient to some degree. This is part of the price we pay for the benefits offered by the market mechanism.[11]

Much is made of the evolutionary argument that noise traders (naïve investors) cannot survive in a competitive market place.[12] To us, the best evidence in favor of the long-term viability of noise traders is the continued existence of active professional arbitrageurs. Ecologists coming upon the African Safari encountered large prides of lions. From the abundance of these predators, they inferred an abundance of gazelles, zebras, and other forms of lion prey. In the same spirit, the massive arbitrage apparatus we observe today attests powerfully to the continuing presence of substantial market imperfections. We cannot at once believe in the existence of lions, and reject the existence of the creatures that are essential to their survival.

Some believe that active asset managers are merely clever marketers, shysters who play no role in making markets more efficient (see, for example, Rubinstein [2001]). But we would then be hard pressed to explain the billions of dollars spent, year after year, in this futile pursuit. Index funds are not a new idea. Why should it take so long for

---

[11] Shleifer [2000] makes this argument, and contains a good discussion of the origins of the efficient market hypothesis.

[12] See Friedman [1953] for the original argument. DeLong et al. [1990a] offer a defense for the survival of noise traders in equilibrium.

investment money to flow to these funds? The same evolutionary forces that are used to argue for the extinction of noise traders, argue also for the extinction of active money managers. Both seem equally puzzling. Either our financial markets have a persistent need to be corrected every year, the magnitude of which runs into the billions of dollars, or the labor market for investment talent is absurdly inefficient.

The fact that active managers do not beat their benchmarks after management fees is often cited as evidence in favor of the efficiency of financial markets. But this evidence has little bearing on the market efficiency debate. The average performance of active managers tells us more about the state of labor markets than about the efficiency of financial markets. If active managers consistently under (over) perform their benchmarks after management fees, capital would flow to passive (active) investment instruments. In equilibrium, the fees they charge should equal the amount of mispricing they remove through their arbitrage activities. We should therefore expect the *after-fee* performance of active managers to approximately equal their benchmark.

How large is the market for active asset management? The answer is not straightforward. It needs to be estimated through multiple sources, and is dependent on fluctuating market prices. As of the end of 2012, a reasonable estimate of the total assets under management (AUM) controlled by professional managers across all asset classes is around 90 trillion USD.[13] Although not all of this AUM is actively managed, multiple sources indicate that the vast majority (at least 70%) resides with active, not passive, managers.[14] Assuming just a flat 1% active

---

[13]Estimates of AUM vary depending on source. A Boston Consulting Group study [Shub et al., 2013] estimates the conventional publicly traded assets managed professionally for fees (pension funds, insurance funds, and mutual funds) to be around US$62.4 trillion at the end of 2012. The City UK Fund Management Report Hines [2012] uses a broader AUM definition, and estimates conventional assets under management to be $85.2 trillion at the end of 2012. This report also provides an estimate of alternative assets (managed by sovereign wealth funds, hedge funds, private equity funds, exchange-traded funds, and wealthy individuals or family offices). Taken together, the CityUK report estimates total assets under global fund management to be $120 trillion.

[14]See for example, Chart 23 in the Hines report, which details the breakdown between active versus passive management by industry sector in the UK.

management fee (not counting performance fees), a conservative estimate of the first-order costs of informational arbitrage is over 600 billion USD per year. This is simply the management fee paid to active managers, who are part of a much larger ecosystem that also includes various other information intermediaries (for example, the prime brokers, sell-side analysts, financial consultants, providers of analytical software, and trading platforms), as well as data vendors (for example, Bloomberg, Thompson-Reuters, Factset, and S&P Capital IQ). Clearly informational arbitrage is big business. Whatever you may think about market efficiency, one thing is certain — the current level of efficiency that we enjoy is the result of a costly price discovery apparatus.

It is difficult to understand how an industry of this size can survive unless, on average, the amount of mispricing extracted by these active managers is on the same order of magnitude. Even if *part* of what we pay for active managers is excessive, it's unlikely that *all* of this expenditure is non-productive. If a significant proportion of active asset managers earn their keep (that is, match or beat their benchmark *after* expenses), their continued survival implies that equilibrium arbitrage costs are huge. We might argue about the speed and precision with which prices incorporate information, but we should not forget the price we pay to achieve it.

1.6   Costly informational arbitrage

Once we view informational arbitrage as a technology, the focus shifts from a macro view of market equilibrium to a micro view of how and when we might recognize mispricings, and what it would take to exploit them. In recent years, a controversial new technology known as "fracking" has revolutionized the energy industry. By allowing trapped natural gas from shale formations to be extracted at much lower costs, fracking has changed the economics of global energy production. Like energy production, active management involves a technology, and all technologies are subject to continuous improvement. Thus a proper understanding of market efficiency can only come when we are willing to examine, and to challenge, the current state of technology for alpha extraction. This is the study of the costly informational arbitrage.

Accounting researchers can contribute to this process by developing lower cost techniques for market arbitrage. For example, our research might lead to better techniques for spotting arbitrage opportunities, thus allowing prices to assimilate the information faster or in a more unbiased manner. Our work might also help to deliver the same level of arbitrage service at a reduced cost. In either case, we improve the efficiency of financial markets by enhancing the cost-effectiveness of the arbitrage mechanism.

Our point is that to improve informational efficiency, we do not need to beat the market *before* active management fees. We can also contribute to the process by reducing the costs of arbitrage. A number of academic studies in accounting have had a substantial impact on the trading behavior of professional arbitrageurs.[15] Perhaps market prices are adjusting more quickly and in a more unbiased fashion as a result of this research. But even if this research has not resulted in more efficient prices, it has almost certainly reduced search costs for arbitrageurs.[16] In this sense, accounting research has directly contributed to the allocation efficiency of financial markets.

Less directly, our educational endeavors also help facilitate this process. Through our classroom efforts, we supply the market with a group of more informed investors. As the level of sophistication improves among market participants, prices also become more efficient. Traditionally, we have in mind the notion that prices are set by the mystical "marginal investor." We do not know who this marginal investor is, but we presume she is quite sophisticated. Yet the evidence on noise trading (discussed in Sections 2 and 3) suggests that relatively unsophisticated investors can also affect returns in market segments they dominate. If

---

[15]For example, Bernard and Thomas [1990], Sloan [1996], Frankel and Lee [1998], Richardson et al. [2005], and Piotroski [2004]. All these studies have been analyzed and used by quant funds, and indeed seem to be reflected in the trading patterns of short sellers — a particularly sophisticated segment of the investing populous [Drake et al., 2011]. See Richardson et al. [2010] for a survey of recent literature in accounting anomalies.

[16]As a testimony to the usefulness of academic research, today hedge funds routinely receive monthly reports from sell-side firms that scour academic sources and summarize key findings for the investment community. One such provider claims to read and filter over 500 studies per month [DBEQS Global, 2014].

we regard price as a capital-weighted consensus of investor opinions, an improvement in the overall sophistication of the investing public results in better markets.

1.7 The "As If" defense of market efficiency

A common assertion is that even if the EMH is not strictly true, it is sufficient to serve as a starting point for research purposes. Like Newtonian physics, it is more than good enough for everyday usage. This is sometimes referred to as the "as if" defense for market efficiency. Unfortunately, it has becoming increasingly more difficult to accommodate what we know about the behavior of prices and returns within this traditional framework. In this subsection, we discuss some of the main practical problems with assuming that price is equal to value.

1.7.1 Trading volume

One immediate problem is trading volume. If we assume price fully reflects all information about future dividends (that is, if equilibrium price is fully revealing), the rational expectations literature suggests that we should have no trading in individual stocks (see, for example, Grossman and Stiglitz [1980]). Black observes:

> *A person with information or insights about individual firms will want to trade, but will realize that only another person with information or insights will take the other side of the trade. Taking the other side's information into account, is it still worth trading? From the point of view of someone who knows what both traders know, one side or the other must be making a mistake. If the one who is making a mistake declines to trade, there must be no trading on information. In other words, I do not believe it makes sense to create a model with information trading but no noise trading.* [Black, 1986, p. 531]

On a typical day, many billions of shares exchange hands at the New York Stock Exchange (NYSE), the Nasdaq, and the NYSE MKT (formerly AMEX). The vast majority of this trading is in individual securities. This enormous appetite for trading individual securities is a challenge for the traditional model, in which price fully reflects information about future dividends.

1.7.2   Volatility

If volume is difficult to explain, volatility is even more problematic.[17] In the classical framework, it is impossible for events that have no information content about future fundamentals to affect prices. Yet empirically, we find that news about fundamentals explains only a fraction of the volatility in returns (see, for example, Roll [1988], Cutler et al. [1989], and Chen et al. [2013]; for anecdotal evidence, witness the October 1987 crash or the daily volatility in internet stocks). In Cutler et al. [1989], for example, macro-economic news variables from past, present, and future periods (for example, innovations in production, consumption, and interest rates) collectively explain less than 50% of the annual variability in stock returns. The same message is echoed in many cross-sectional studies that attempt to explain stock returns with accounting-based fundamentals (see, for example, Easton et al. [1992] and Richardson et al. [2012]).[18] Throughout this literature, we find stock prices seem to move for reasons that have little to do with fundamental news. The weight of this evidence behooves us to adopt

---

[17]Using a variance bound test, Shiller [1981a,b] examined the proposition that stock prices are too volatile and concluded in the affirmative. This study precipitated a debate over the correction needed for variance calculations when both dividends and stock prices follow highly persistent processes with unit roots [see Kleidon, 1986, Marsh and Merton, 1986, Campbell and Shiller, 1987, 1988a,b]. In particular, Campbell and Shiller [1987] tested a form of the dividend discount model that modifies the variance calculation for the unit root case, and once again found excessive volatility. See Campbell [2014] for a good discussion of this topic.

[18]In Easton et al. [1992], fundamental accounting variables explain 15% and 5% of the cross-sectional returns for two- and one-year horizons, respectively. Even when using a 10-year window, the authors find the adjusted r-square between stock returns and accounting measures to be only 62%. In a more recent study, Richardson et al. [2012] include both firms' expected returns and forward-looking fundamental news (using analyst forecasts of earnings), and find that collectively these variables explain less than 40% of the variance in annual stock returns.

a broader view of asset-pricing, and to entertain the possibility that other forces are at work in shaping prices and returns.

1.7.3   Return predictability

Third, the evidence on the predictability of stock returns is increasingly more difficult to reconcile with the efficient market framework.[19] With risk-averse investors, all tests of potential trading strategies are a joint test of an asset-pricing model. If the asset-pricing model is misspecified, it is always possible that the abnormal returns are some form of compensation for yet another unknown risk factor. However, with many of the more recent pricing anomalies, the risk-based explanations are becoming less plausible because of the ancillary evidence associated with these findings.

We find particularly compelling the evidence that *healthier* and *safer* firms, as measured by various measures of risk or fundamentals, often earn higher subsequent returns. Firms with lower Beta, lower volatility, lower distress risk, lower leverage, and superior measures of profitability and growth, all earn higher returns (see, for example, Dichev [1998], Piotroski [2000], Lakonishok et al. [1994], and Asness et al. [2013]). If these firms are riskier, it is odd that they should exhibit future operating and return characteristics that suggest the opposite. We discuss this evidence in more detail in Sections 4 and 6.

The finding that a substantial portion of the abnormal returns is earned around subsequent earnings release dates is also extremely difficult to explain in a risk context.[20] Asset-pricing models do not predict these short-window price moves. Finally, the so-called momentum studies, that document subsequent price drifts to various corporate news releases (including earnings surprises, dividend announcements, and stock splits), are particularly difficult to reconcile with risk-based

---

[19]Much of this evidence has been discussed in prior survey work (see, for example, Fama [1991], Shleifer [2000], Kothari [2001], and Richardson et al. [2010]).

[20]Bernard and Thomas [1990] was perhaps the first and best-known study to use this technique in distinguishing between risk and mispricing explanations. Richardson et al. [2010] contain a good discussion.

explanations.[21] The fact that these events predict subsequent earnings surprises and the direction of analyst earnings revisions suggests that they are related to market misperceptions of earnings rather than risk (see, for example, La Porta [1996], Chan et al. [1996], and Richardson et al. [2010]).

It might be worthwhile to note the evolving nature of the evidence in this literature over time. Initially, much effort was focused on *documenting* apparent pricing anomalies (see, for example, DeBondt and Thaler [1985, 1987]). More recent efforts have been focused on *explaining* these anomalies and testing various behavioral models (see, for example, Arif and Lee [2015]), sometimes using experimental techniques [Libby et al., 2002]. We believe that future studies along these lines will not merely document new anomalies, but will also help to explain them. The literature is still at an early stage of development, but what we know is sufficient to convince many that risk-based explanations alone are not enough.

1.7.4 Cost-of-capital

Finally, one of the most elemental challenges to the efficient market paradigm is spawned by the cost of capital dilemma. Historically, asset-pricing models have been tested using average realized returns to proxy for expected returns. This practice is based on the assumption that market prices are unbiased in large samples. Yet even this weaker form of market efficiency has been questioned in recent times. As Elton [1999] observes in his presidential address to the American Finance Association, "(t)here are periods longer than 10 years during which stock market realized returns are on average less than the risk-free rate (1973 to 1984). There are periods longer than 50 years in which risky long-term bonds on average underperform the risk free rate (1927 to 1981)."

In other words, historical realized returns do not appear to be an appropriate proxy for expected returns, even averaged over decades.

---

[21]Ikenberry and Ramnath [2002] summarize the evidence on post-event drifts. Asness and Liew [2014] provide a good discussion of value and momentum strategies, as well as a practitioner's take on the market efficiency debate.

Changing risk premiums and conditional asset-pricing theories are likely to explain some time-series variations, but these explanations cannot account for risky assets earning persistently lower returns than the risk-free rate. Indeed, growing discontent with the noisy nature of average realized returns is the main impetus for the move toward valuation-based techniques for estimating expected returns (see, for example, Claus and Thomas [2000], Gebhardt et al. [2001], or Fama and French [2002]). Once again, we find that the "price equals value" assumption fails the Newtonian test of practical usage.

Summary

The main point of this section is that, as researchers, we need to think about fundamental ("intrinsic") value and the current market price as two distinct measures. This is because the problems engendered by the naïve view of market efficiency expressed in equation (1) are simply too pervasive to ignore. In fact, we believe the unshackling of price from value is a key conceptual step toward a better understanding of many long-standing puzzles in empirical financial economics, including: excessive trading volume, excessive return volatility, the pervasive evidence on returns predictability, the cost of capital dilemma, and the continued existence of a large active asset management industry.

At each point in the information aggregation process, Price is informed by, but not confined to equal, Value. In fact, the possibility of mispricing is what gives market participants the incentive to uncover news about firm value. This is an extremely important concept to get across to researchers working in the capital market area. Indeed, we view it as the "watershed" shift in thinking needed to bridge academic researchers with most asset managers.

A second central point made in this section is the need to focus on the market for information, and not merely the market for the assets themselves. The size of the active asset management industry speaks powerfully to the importance and complexity of the information market. In our view, the market for information deserves at least as much attention as the market for the assets themselves. Economic incentives, behavioral biases, and other frictions in the market for information are keys to better understanding of the pricing problems in the market for the underlying assets. In short, informational arbitrage is a costly and complex process that deserves more academic attention. This is a recurrent theme throughout the book.

2

The Noise Trader Approach to Finance: An Alternative to the EMH?

This section discusses the role of noise traders in market dynamics and pricing by examining in some detail a simple noise trader model (NTM) from Shiller [1984].[1] In many ways, this is an early prototype of more sophisticated behavioral models that appear later. Shiller himself acknowledges this model is "no doubt oversimplified and restrictive" (p. 477). Nevertheless, as we show below, the conceptual kernel of the model remains intact, and it is as relevant to the field of behavioral finance today as when it was first introduced. In fact, the ideas introduced in this model largely foreshadowed the central themes that will emerge in behavioral finance in subsequent decades.

We present the Shiller model as an important alternative to the EMH for understanding market-pricing dynamics. A particularly attractive feature of the model is the way it integrates the three key elements in the formation of security prices: (1) firm fundamentals, (2) investor sentiment, and (3) arbitrage costs. The model does so by explicitly including costly informational arbitrage (although Shiller

---

[1]In brief "noise trading" refers to the net demand for an asset that is not based on an optimal forecast of the present value of its expected future cash flows. This term is discussed in more detail later in the section.

does not use this term). Because arbitrage is costly in this model, mispricing becomes an equilibrium phenomenon. As a result, market prices are informed by, but not constrained to, firm fundamentals.

To us, the noise trader approach to finance in general (and the Shiller framework in particular) provides a much more reasonable starting point for classes on financial statement analysis and equity valuation than the EMH. Unlike a naïve form of the EMH, the noise trader approach anticipates costly information acquisition, and thus a role for some individuals to expend resources in acquiring a better understanding of firm fundamentals. At the same time, it recognizes noise trader activities impose a risk on all investors, and that this risk increases the cost-of-capital for everyone in equilibrium.

Both costly information and noise trader risk are essential features of a market in which a subset of investors engage in fundamental analysis and informational arbitrage. In contrast, in a world where markets are efficient and informational costs are trivial, it would be difficult to understand why information gathering and analyses might be worthwhile. In balance, it would appear the market depicted by the NTM bears a much stronger resemblance to reality than the market depicted by the EMH.

After presenting the most important features of the Shiller noise trader model, we will discuss its broad implications for market-based research in both accounting and finance. We then use this model as an organizing framework to provide a brief overview of how the behavioral finance literature has developed in the years following Shiller [1984].

2.1 Overview

In his spirited defense of market efficiency, Rubinstein [2001] makes reference to what he calls *The Prime Directive* for financial economists:

> *Explain asset prices by rational models. Only if all attempts fail, resort to irrational investor behavior.* [Rubinstein, 2001, p. 16] (emphasis is ours).

Rubinstein complains that the "burgeoning behavioralist literature…
has lost all the constraints of this directive — that whatever anomalies
are discovered, illusory or not, behavioralists will come up with an
explanation grounded in systematic irrational investor behavior." (p. 4)
This is an often-heard complaint against the behavioral camp. But it
is an unfair complaint, because behavioral models today do not need
to violate this prime directive.

Most models in behavioral finance today feature noise traders and
constrained arbitrage. We refer to them as "rational behavioral models"
because they accommodate rational arbitrage, with explicit cost constraints.[2] Such models feature a set of agents ("smart money" traders)
who are able to make rational forecasts of firm values. However, these
rational agents are faced with a set of cost constraints, and also need
to contend with the effects of noise trading. The Shiller [1984] model is
one of the earliest examples of this approach to characterizing market-
pricing dynamics.

2.1.1 Who are noise traders?

A distinguishing feature of rational behavioral models is that they feature noise traders. Fischer Black's influential Presidential address to
the American Finance Association contains the following definition of
noise traders:

> *Noise trading is trading on noise as if it were information.*
> *People who trade on noise are willing to trade even though*
> *from an objective point of view they would be better off not*
> *trading. Perhaps they think the noise they are trading on*

---

[2]There is now a large theoretical literature in behavioral asset-pricing. We have
in mind studies such as: Barberis et al. [1998], Hong and Stein [1999], Daniel
et al. [1998, 2001], Barberis and Huang [2008], Barberis et al. [2001], Barberis
and Shleifer [2003], Barberis and Huang [2008], Eyster et al. [2013] and Barberis
et al. [2015]. Earlier works along these lines include Shiller [1984], and DeLong
et al. [1990a,b]. See Barberis and Thaler [2002], Hirshleifer [2001], Baker and Wurgler [2007], and Barberis [2013] for good summaries. All these models feature noise
traders and constrained arbitrage.

> *is information. Or perhaps they just like to trade.* [Black, 1986, p. 531]

In short, we are a noise trader whenever we act on a signal that ultimately proves to be value-irrelevant. Under this definition, the existence of noise traders is as intuitive as it is innocuous. With continuous information flows, it is improbable that all traders can instantaneously calibrate the quality of their own signals. In this world, informed investors making ex ante rational trades may nevertheless lose money ex post on any given trade. Even if these investors are right more often than they are wrong, they are frequently engaged in noise trading. The existence of noise traders is therefore not inconsistent with the prime directive. In fact, noise trading is a necessary part of the price discovery process.

As Black [1986] observes, noise trading is the "missing ingredient" in the traditional model. Noise trading helps to explain the enormous volume of trading we observe daily. Noise trading is the driving force behind much of the volatility in realized returns. Noise trading explains the continued existence of arbitrage. Finally, noise trading, in concert with the costly nature of arbitrage, helps to explain why prices can deviate sharply, and for persistent periods of time, away from fundamental value.

2.2   The Shiller model

In the standard rational expectation equilibrium, the real (inflation adjusted) rate of return on a stock between time t and time $t+1$ may be defined as: $R_t = (P_{t+1} - P_t + D_t)/P_t$, where P_t is the real price of the share at time t and D_t is real dividend paid, if any, during the time period. In this setting, assuming future returns are unforecastable, we can further represent the expected return for a stock over period t by a constant, $E_t[R_t] = \delta$, where $E_t[\ ]$ is the mathematical expectation conditional on all publicly available information at time t. Subject to weak assumptions about the stability of terminal conditions, we can then derive the following[3]

$$P_t = \sum_{k=0}^{\infty} \frac{E_t[D_{t+k}]}{(1+\delta)^{k+1}} \tag{2.1}$$

This is, of course, a familiar expression of real price as the discounted present value of expected future dividends, taking into account all publicly available information at time t.

Shiller's alternative model begins with the same setup, but assumes the existence of two types of agents: "smart-money" investors and "noise traders" (whom Shiller also refers to as "ordinary investors"). Smart-money investors trade on the basis of fundamental information, but their actions are subject to wealth constraints, meaning that they do not have unlimited, instantaneous, and persistent access to capital as commonly assumed under traditional asset-pricing models. These investors respond to news about fundamental value quickly and in an unbiased manner and value shares according to Equation (1). Noise traders, on the other hand, include everyone who does not trade on the basis of an optimal response to news about fundamentals.

Notationally, the demands of these two types of traders can be expressed as follows:

Noise Traders (Ordinary Investors)

These investors have time-varying demands, not based on expected returns optimally forecasted. The valuation that ordinary investors ascribe to each share is denoted by Y_t and the total value of their demand equals $Y_t * S_t$, where S_t is the total number of shares outstanding.

Information Traders (Smart money)

The demand for shares by smart money at time t expressed as a portion of total shares outstanding and denoted as: $Q_t = (E_t[R_t] - \rho)/\phi$,

---

[3]To solve for Equation (1), note that $P_t = bE_t[P_t] + bE_t[P_{t+1}]$, where $b = 1/(1+\delta)$. Given $Et[Et_{+k}] = E_t$ for all $k > 0$, we can substitute for P_{t+1} and obtain $P_t = bE_t[D_{t+1}] + b^2E_t[P_{t+2}]$. If we repeat this process, successively substituting for the price terms on the right-hand side, we will obtain Equation (1). The terminal condition assumption needed is that the price term, $b_nE_t[P_{t+n}]$, goes to zero as n goes to infinity. See Shiller [1984] for details.

where R_t is the real rate of return on the stock at time t, $\rho =$ the expected real return such that there is no demand for shares by smart money, and $\phi =$ the expected compensation rate that would induce smart money to hold all the shares. Thus, a time t expected return of $E_t[R_t] = \rho + \phi$ would induce smart money to demand 100% of shares outstanding (that is, $Q_t = 1$). This identity shows that ϕ can be interpreted as the minimum expected return "premium" above ρ that would induce smart money to hold all shares. Moreover, the total value of smart money demand equals $Q_t * S_t * P_t$.

In equilibrium, the market clears when supply equals demand. This occurs when the market price, P_t, causes the total value of smart money demand and noise trader demand to equal the total value of shares outstanding: $Q_t*S_t*P_t+Y_t*S_t = S_t*P_t$ (that is, when $Q_t+(Y_t/P_t) = 1$). Solving for the resulting rational expectation equilibrium recursively in the same manner as for Equation (1) yields the following market-clearing price:

$$P_t = \sum_{k=0}^{\infty} \frac{E_t[D_{t+k}] + \phi E_t[Y_{t+k}]}{(1 + \rho + \phi)^{k+1}} \qquad (2.2)$$

Expressed in this form, the market price is the present value, discounted at rate $(1 + \rho + \phi)$, of the expected future dividend payments at time t (that is, $E_t[D_{t+k}]$), plus ϕ times the expected future demand by noise traders ($E_t[Y_{t+k}]$). In other words, P_t is jointly determined by a firm's fundamental value (future dividends) and a more capricious factor (future noise trader demand).

Notice that the relative importance of the two factors is determined by ϕ. Recall that ϕ is the premium above ρ that would induce the smart money to hold all the shares. This term can be loosely interpreted as a measure of the cost of arbitrage, because smaller values of ϕ result in greater demands from smart money to trade against expected mispricing (that is, $E_t[R_t] - \rho$).

Notice that as ϕ approaches zero, the market price in Equation (2) becomes a function of expected dividends, and the efficient market model (Equation (1)) emerges as a special case. In other words, in markets where costs of arbitrage are low, prices behave much as predicted by the efficient market hypothesis. However, as ϕ increases, so does the relative importance of noise trading. In the extreme, as ϕ approaches infinity, the market price is determined solely by noise trader demand, and fundamental valuation plays a trivial role in setting prices. Thus in the NTM, the EMH is a special case where arbitrage costs are close to zero.

What factors might affect arbitrage costs (ϕ)? The Shiller model is silent on this, but one might reasonably surmise empirical proxies that capture the costs and risks faced by active investors engaged in informational arbitrage would reflect the spirit of this parameter. Clearly characteristics of smart-money investors, such as the level of their risk aversion and their wealth or funding constraint, would be important. More generally, active managers often speak of arbitrage costs in terms of: (1) *trading costs*: costs associated with establishing and closing the position; including brokerage fees, price slippage, bid–ask spreads, etc., (2) *holding costs*: costs associated with sustaining a position; these costs are affected by factors such as the duration of the arbitrage position and the incremental cost of short-selling a stock, and (3) *information costs*: costs associated with information acquisition, analysis, and monitoring.[4]

The model predicts that markets in which these types of costs are low will feature prices that are close to fundamentals. For example, the markets for index futures, closed-end funds, and exchange-traded funds are characterized by relatively low transaction and information costs. In these markets, valuation is relatively straightforward, transaction costs are minimal, and the traded assets often have close substitutes. As might be expected, the prices for these assets are closely tied to their fundamental values.[5]

In other markets, however, arbitrage costs (ϕ) can be potentially large, and the model predicts in such markets noise traders activities dominate. For example, the capital markets of emerging economies often feature relatively few fundamental investors, little market liquidity and therefore high arbitrage costs. Even in U.S. markets, smaller

---

[4]Shleifer and Vishny [1997] model the limits of arbitrage. We devote Section 5 to this topic.

[5]Even so, the evidence on closed-end fund discounts suggests that Y_t exists and is mean-reverting (see, for example, Lee et al. [1991]).

firms, less closely followed and less actively traded stocks, and growth stocks that are difficult to value will likely have higher arbitrage costs. The noise trader model predicts that security prices in these markets will display more volatility, and will often seem to bear little relation to their fundamental values.[6]

The main message from this model is that market prices are a product of the interplay between noise traders and rational arbitrageurs, operating under cost constraints. Once we introduce noise traders and costly arbitrage, price is no longer simply a function of future expected dividends. Unless arbitrage costs are zero, P_t will not generally equal V_t. The magnitude of the mispricing is a function of noise trader demand and arbitrage costs. More generally, when arbitrage costs are non-zero, we can expect some mispricing to be an equilibrium phenomenon.

Another key insight is that the unpredictability of returns (a "no free lunch" version of the efficient market hypothesis) does not guarantee price equals value (a "the price is right" version of the efficient market hypothesis). Unfortunately, when the efficient market hypothesis is invoked, it is often in the latter form. The fact that returns are largely unpredictable has been widely interpreted as evidence in support of the fact that price equals the present value of expected dividends. However, the model illustrates a conceptual problem with this general approach to testing for market efficiency. In the model, returns may be unpredictable but stock prices can still diverge dramatically from fundamental values.[7]

Finally, the model highlights the difference between fundamental analysis and security analysis. Fundamental analysis is concerned with measuring firm value regardless of market conditions. But in making

---

[6]Subsequent work by Baker and Wurgler [2006] provide strong support for this aspect of the Shiller model. Specifically, Baker and Wurgler show that, in the cross-section, a firm's sensitivity to a measure of market-wide sentiment (that is, its "Sentiment Beta") is indeed a function of arbitrage costs (measured by its idiosyncratic volatility).

[7]For example, if arbitrage is costly (that is, $\phi > 0$) and noise trader demand (Y_t) follows a random walk, the second term in the numerator can be large, but stock returns are unpredictable. More generally, if Y_t exhibits long-horizon mean-reversion, rational traders with finite horizons would not be able to exploit the mispricing, even if it is currently large.

security selections, smart-money investors need to consider the behavior of noise traders, as well as fundamental valuation, in determining their own strategy. Smart money investors need to consider "fashions" and "fads" in addition to "fundamentals." Moreover, the time-series behavior of Y_t becomes important. If noise trader demand is random, then P_t is still the best forecast of V_t. However, if Y_t is mean reverting, then fundamental analysis is potentially profitable. We expand on this point in the next section.

2.3 The noise trader approach to finance

It has now been three decades since Shiller published his model. In the ensuing years, behavioral finance has continued to grow and expand as a subfield of economics. Interestingly, the key features of this model have endured, and continue to be a useful organizing framework for much of the subsequent work.

Today, work on the "noise trader approach to finance" [see Shleifer and Summers, 1990] continues along three lines: (1) Investor sentiment (or non-fundamental price pressures), (2) Firm fundamentals (or equity valuation), and (3) Limits to arbitrage. We will take a closer look at each of the three components of the model in the next three sections: Section 3 (Investor Sentiment), Section 4 (Equity Valuation), and Section 5 (Limits to Arbitrage). In the meantime, we present an extremely condensed synopsis of the three strands of research.

2.3.1 Investor sentiment

Broadly defined, investor sentiment refers to "optimism" (or "pessimism") not justified by existing fundamentals. Shiller envisioned traders who overreact/underreact to news, or are vulnerable to fads and fashion trends, and much of his original article was devoted to a discussion of noise trading as a social phenomenon. However, because the source of noise is exogenous, what qualifies as investor sentiment in the model is in fact quite broad, and includes for example the actions of those who trade for liquidity or consumption-based reasons. A distinguishing feature of investor sentiment is that it reflects coordinated (or systemic) investor demand of a non-fundamental nature, and thus the price pressure it generates will cause price to move away from fundamental value.[8]

Subsequent empirical studies have used various techniques to measure market-wide sentiment. Examples included the discount on closed-end funds [Lee et al., 1991], the proportion of equity vs. debt issues by corporations [Baker and Wurgler, 2000], the consumer confidence index [Lemmon and Portniaguina, 2006], the monthly fund flow between equity and bond mutual funds within the same family Ben-Rephael et al. [2012], and a bottom–up measure of aggregate corporate investment [Arif and Lee, 2015], and a composite sentiment index [Baker and Wurgler, 2006, Baker et al., 2012]. See Baker and Wurgler [2007] for a good summary.

Although investor sentiment is often viewed as a market-wide phenomenon, the concept of non-fundamental price pressure is also highly relevant to the relative pricing of individual securities, industries (for example, e-commerce or biotech), geographical regions, or investment "styles" (for example, value versus growth, or low-volatility versus high-volatility). When certain stocks, industries, regions, or styles of investing become "hot", money flows in that direction, resulting in initial price escalations, followed by subsequent return reversals [Barberis and Shleifer, 2003].

A particularly interesting line of research examines the net inflows of money into mutual funds. The investor clientele of mutual funds is almost entirely retail in nature. At the same time, mutual fund managers' buy/sell decisions are strongly affected by whether their funds are experiencing net inflows or net outflows. Consistent with behavioral explanations featuring retail investor sentiment, a number of studies have found that "flow induced trading" by mutual funds lead to predictable future return patterns among stocks being held by these funds (see, for example, Coval and Stafford [2007], Frazzini and Lamont [2008], and Lou [2012]). Indeed, we now have substantial evidence

---

[8]Unless noise trading is positively correlated across traders, or systemic, it will not affect price. Empirically, trading records from individual brokerage accounts suggest that noise trading is indeed systemic (see, for example, Kumar and Lee [2006]).

that mutual fund trades are on average price destabilizing [Puckett and Yan, 2013, Arif et al., 2015]. Several studies also show that investor sentiment as measure by these retail flows have an effect on real corporate decisions taken by managers [Khan et al., 2012, Arif and Lee, 2015].

More broadly, the literature on investor sentiment has examined the effect of signal saliency and statistical reliability on the proclivity of investors to over- and under-weight individual signals. Following the lead of psychologists (see, for example, Kahneman and Tversky [1974] and Griffin and Tversky [1992]), researchers have observed a broad tendency for investors to over-weight signals that are more salient or attention grabbing (see, for example, Barber and Odean [2008], Hirshleifer et al. [2009], Da et al. [2011], and Engelberg et al. [2012b]), and under-weight signals that are statistically reliable but less salient, or required more processing to be understood (see, for example, Della Vigna and Pollet [2007], Gleason and Lee [2003], Giglio and Shue [2014], Cohen and Lou [2012], Cohen et al. [2013a,b]).

In sum, the literature on investor sentiment is vast. We will cover it in far more detail in Section 3 and will touch on it again when discussing value investing (Section 4). At this point, our main message to accounting researchers is that stock prices can move for many reasons other than a change in the present value of its expected future cash flows. These movements can be large and persistent without being exploitable. Yet far from reducing the relevance of fundamental analysis, this observation about markets actually elevates its importance.

2.3.2 Equity valuation

A large literature examines the measurement of firm value based on fundamental analysis. Much of the innovation has taken place in accounting in recent years, where the re-emergence of the residual income model (RIM) has been central in the advancement of this research agenda.[9] Although this line of inquiry is not typically associated with

---

[9]RIM had its origin in the early work of financial economists (see, for example, Preinreich [1938], Edwards and Bell [1961], Peasnell [1982], and Lehman [1993]). In the mid-1990s, a series of influential studies by James Ohlson [Ohlson, 1990, 1991, 1995, Feltham and Ohlson, 1995] helped accounting researchers to focus sharply

behavioral finance, it fits well within the Shiller framework. In the context of a noisy market price, an independent assessment of firm value based on sustainable expected cash flows becomes central. Indeed, unless and until we have a sensible measure of the value of firms based on expected payoffs to shareholders, it is difficult to empirically distinguish between the two terms in the numerator of Equation (1).

In Section 4 of this volume, we provide a review of some key insights gleaned from accounting-based valuation theory. Our analysis demonstrates the inextricable conceptual link between a stock's "cheapness" (what the finance literature refers to as "the value effect", typically measured using various market multiples), and its "quality" (what the accounting fraternity sometimes refers to as "fundamental pricing anomalies", but which we believe are simply accounting-based indicators of firm's expected growth opportunities).

A key prediction of Shiller's model is that, if arbitrage costs are non-trivial, sharper measures of firm value will yield superior predictive power for future returns. As we show in Section 3, an enormous body of evidence now suggests this is indeed the case.

2.3.3 Limits to arbitrage

The third element in the Shiller model is arbitrage costs (represented by ϕ). In equilibrium rational investors are compensated not only for bearing fundamental risk, but also for costs and risks associated with noise trading. Subsequent analytical studies have provided more structure by modelling various aspects of the costs faced by informational arbitrageurs, including: agency problems raising from delegated asset management [Shleifer and Vishny, 1997], noise trader risk [DeLong et al., 1990a,b], and a coordination problem faced by even sophisticated investors [Stein, 2009].

More broadly, arbitrage costs encompass all costs and risks related to the exploitation of price deviations from fundamental value. Once

---

on the importance of the model as a means to understanding the relation between accounting data and firm value. Another key contributor to this research has been Columbia professor Stephen Penman (see, for example, Penman [1997, 2010, 2012]).

again, the idea of arbitrage costs is applicable at the market level, the industry level, the style level, or the individual security level. At the individual security level, Baker and Wurgler [2006] operationalize this concept using firm-level idiosyncratic volatility as an empirical proxy. Many other studies have documented a relationship between arbitrage constraints and the magnitude of security mispricings (see, for example, Pontiff [1996], Mendenhall [2004], and Mashruwala et al. [2006]). The role of short selling has received particular attention (see, for example, Blocher et al. [2013], Beneish et al. [2015], and Hirshleifer et al. [2011b]).

Increasingly, we find evidence that market frictions can have a dramatic effect on the pricing of assets. For example, even in extremely liquid markets, such as monthly Treasury auctions, dealers' limited risk-bearing capacity and end-investors' imperfect capital mobility can impact prices and cause predictable patterns in future returns [Lou et al., 2013]. The influence of market frictions on prices is also highly time varying. For example, So and Wang [2014] provide evidence that short-term return reversals in equity markets, a proxy for the expected return market makers demand for providing liquidity, increase over sixfold immediately prior to earnings announcements due to increased inventory risks associated with holding net positions through the release of anticipated earnings news. At the same time, the ability of market participants to assimilate news seems to be affected by their limited attention span and processing power [Hirshleifer and Teoh, 2003, Hirshleifer et al., 2009].

2.4 Implications for market-based research

We have argued that decoupling fundamental value from price is an important conceptual step toward a richer research agenda. But, if price is not always equal to value, what role should market prices play in our research design? How do we evaluate alternative estimates of value if price is a noisy proxy for fundamental value? What specific areas of research appear particularly promising at the moment? We turn now to these issues.

2.4.1   Suggestions for future research

What type of research will have the greatest impact in the future? Rather than generating a laundry list, we will try to outline several features of salient research. Broadly speaking, we believe the salient research in this area will be: (1) decision-driven, (2) interdisciplinary in nature, and (3) prospective in focus.[10]

Decision-driven. Many young researchers begin their quest for a research topic by reading recent issues of academic journals. Given the lead time to publication at most of our top academic outlets, these journals are not necessarily the best starting point for new research projects. An alternative, and complementary, approach is to begin by identifying significant economic decisions that utilize accounting data. In terms of generating ideas, practitioner journals can be a good place to begin. The aim is to acquire an independent perspective on topics that matter, in a broader economic context, *before* getting too close to the academic literature itself.

Decision-driven research is not to be confused with product development or consulting. We are not suggesting that we direct our research to practitioners. Rather, our call is for more research that is based on careful observation of how decision makers behave, and how information signals are used (or misused). Even basic research aimed at the theoretical foundations of our discipline will benefit from more detailed knowledge of how important economic decisions are made.

Excellent examples of this type of research come from the literature on fundamental analysis. In these studies, accounting-based variables are used to predict a variety of future outcomes. For example, financial statement variables have been used to predict financial distress [Altman, 1968] and future earning changes [Ou and Penman, 1989]. They have proved useful in assessing the persistence of earnings [Sloan, 1996, Richardson et al., 2005], improvements in fundamentals [Piotroski, 2000, Piotroski and So, 2012], and the probability of

---

[10]See Ohlson [2011] for a related discussion on identifying successful research topics. Ohlson [2011] argues that successful research derives from a thorough understanding of the way the world works, rather than from stylized academic theories that likely omit relevant institutional details.

earnings manipulation [Beneish, 1999, Beneish et al., 2013]. Often, these variables also possess predictive power for subsequent stock returns (see Richardson et al., 2010 for a good summary).

Interdisciplinary in nature. Few capital allocation decisions of significance involve solely the use of accounting information. Therefore, it should not be surprising that the most important accounting research in the capital market area will be interdisciplinary in nature. Solid training in finance and economics is essential in these undertakings.

Some of the most interesting topics open to accountants today have traditionally been regarded as the domain of corporate finance, asset-pricing, or behavioral finance, even though accounting information plays an important role in these decision contexts. In our view, accounting researchers are likely to be better qualified to address many issues that arise in equity valuation, share repurchases, LBOs, IPOs, loan syndications, mergers and acquisitions, and stock selection, than their counterparts in finance. If we are willing to tackle these issues, accounting researchers have the opportunity to generate some of the most significant research in financial economics over the next few decades.

In addition, we believe that it is now important for accounting researchers to be familiar with the behavioral finance literature. Thaler [1999] predicts the demise of behavioral finance as a separate branch of finance because he believes that, in the future, all of finance will be behavioral. We are not at that stage yet, but the trend is unmistakably in this direction. In 2012, the *Journal of Financial Economics* had a special issue on the topic of Investor Sentiment, something unthinkable only a few decades ago.

We believe that accountants also have an important role to play in understanding noise trader demand. Unlike Keynes' animal spirits, Shiller's noise traders are not driven primarily by idiosyncratic impulses or "a spontaneous urge to action" Keynes [1936, p. 161]. Instead, the mistakes in investor expectations are correlated across traders. Thus, Shiller does not model individual irrationality so much as mass psychology or clientele effects. A common preference or belief, which we might call investor sentiment, affects large groups of investors at the same time.

What gives rise to these common sentiments (that is, what affects Y_t)? Shiller suggests sentiments arise when investors trade on pseudo-signals, such as price and volume patterns, popular models, or the forecasts of Wall Street gurus. More generally, Y_t captures any price effect other than those arising from the optimal use of dividend-related information. In this sense, noise trader demand can be due to either sub-optimal use of available information, over- and under-reactions to legitimate information signals, or responses to other exogenous liquidity shocks.[11]

The most salient feature of noise trader demand is that it drives price away from a stock's fundamental value. Therefore, as we refine our valuation tools, we simultaneously generate better metrics for measuring noise trader demand. As information economists, accountants can help identify signals (or pseudo-signals) that affect noise trader demand. We can also shed light on the nature and extent of information processing costs (see, for example, Demers and Vega [2011] and Engelberg [2008]), and how these costs impact corporate disclosure decisions [Blankespoor, 2013]. In fact, prior studies in accounting that investigate the under-utilization of information in financial reports (see, for example, Sloan [1996] and Richardson et al. [2005]) can be viewed as efforts to identify noise trader preferences. Once we recognize that we can all be noise traders (that noise traders are not a breed apart), the reconciliation with current accounting research is not difficult.

Prospective in focus. Much of accounting is historical in nature. A good deal of our research in the capital market area has also tended to be retrospective and conducted within a framework where stock return (or price) appears as the dependent variable and contemporaneous accounting data appear as independent variables. According to this widely utilized paradigm, accounting data that better explain contemporaneous returns (or prices) are presumed to be superior in some normative sense.

---

[11]In the noisy rational expectation literature, the noise introduced by exogenous liquidity shocks is crucial in inducing trading and in limiting the extent to which price reveals full information. For an example of this type of model, see Grossman and Stiglitz [1980] or Diamond and Verrecchia [1981].

However, as pointed out by Bernard [1995, p. 743], this paradigm is limiting because it "precludes *from the outset* the possibility that researchers could ever discover something that was not already known by the market." As our view on market efficiency changes, we believe a greater emphasis will be placed on research that helps predict the outcome of *future* economic events. This research will have as a primary focus the goal of enhancing capital allocation decisions whose outcomes are not yet known. It will include, but not be limited to, studies that help to forecast future stock returns.

Each year the American Accounting Association (AAA) awards a Notable Contributions to Accounting Literature Award. The recipient(s) of this award have written, in the view of the selection committee, the most influential study in accounting over the past five years. The subject matters covered by the past winners are diverse, and include: earnings quality, cost-of-capital, equity valuation, financial statement analysis, managerial accounting, auditor judgment, international accounting standards, and corporate governance.[12] But even a cursory review of these winners will make plain the importance of focusing on decision-relevant and interdisciplinary research of a prospective nature.

2.5 Research design issues

If the stock price itself is a noisy measure for a firm's true fundamental value, how should we proceed in designing our research studies? How do we model the relation between value and price? This is a matter of obvious import as we leave the comfortable confines of the efficient market paradigm. Future researchers will need to grapple with this matter more thoroughly, but the following two empirical studies might serve to illustrate the possibilities. Both are what we regard as "hybrid" studies that do not discard the information in market price completely, but rely on weaker assumptions about the relation between price and fundamental value.

---

[12]See http://aaahq.org/awards/awrd3win.htm.

First, Lee et al. [LMS, 1999] models price and value as a co-integrated system — in other words, the observed price and the accountant's estimate of value both measure the true (but unobservable) fundamental value with noise. In this context, they examine the question of how value estimates based on accounting numbers should be evaluated. They show that in this framework, under fairly general conditions, superior value estimates will not only be more correlated with contemporaneous returns, but will also yield better predictions of future returns.

In the LMS model, prices and value are assumed to be long-term convergent due to arbitrage forces. However, in the spirit of the noise trader model discussed in the prior section, at any given point in time market price can diverge from the true (but unobserved) fundamental value. In this context, the role of fundamental analysis is to generate an independent value estimate that helps to discipline the observed price. Their analysis suggests two benchmarks for evaluating the degree to which an accountant's empirical value estimate has been successful in capturing true fundamental value. Specifically, LMS argues that superior measures of true intrinsic value will be better able to: (a) track price variation over time, and (b) predict of future returns.[13] Using these two performance metrics, they provide evidence on the usefulness of various inputs into the RIM model — such as analyst forecasts, time-varying discount rates, etc.

Second, Gebhardt et al. [GLS, 2001] use a discounted residual income model to generate a market implied cost-of-capital. They then examine firm characteristics that are systematically related to this cost-of-capital estimate. They show that a firm's implied cost-of-capital is a function of its industry membership, B/M ratio, forecasted long-term growth rate, and the dispersion in analyst earnings forecasts and use these firm characteristics to estimate an "expected" or "warranted" cost-of-capital for each firm. Due to this warranted approach, the research design in GLS is not based on an assumption of market

---

[13] Tests of mean reversion rates between price and value are extensively used in the literature on macroeconomic finance and referred to as error correction models (see, for example, Miller [1991] and Malpezzi [1999]).

efficiency in the traditional sense (that is, $P_t = V_t, \forall t$) nor does it rely on a firm's current market price. For purposes of stock selection, it would be tautological to estimate the implied cost-of-capital based on current stock prices. Rather, GLS relies on long-term relations between the market implied cost-of-capital and various firm characteristics. This warranted cost-of-capital is then compared with the "actual implied" cost-of-capital derived from the current price. Trading strategies are based on the "spread" between the warranted and actual measures.[14]

Both LMS and GLS implicitly assume a weaker form of market efficiency than is commonly found in the literature. Specifically, these studies assume that price and value are locked together in the long run by arbitrage forces. Price contains valuable information about future payoffs that should not be ignored. However, at any given point in time, price also departs from fundamental value due to exogenous forces (or, in the parlance of behavioral finance, noise trader demand).

The authors in these studies exploit the long-term relation between accounting fundamentals and market prices to gauge short-term price deviations. We refer to this as a "hybrid" approach, because it utilizes both accounting fundamentals and past prices to predict future prices. Returning to the ocean analogy, these studies use the *average* level of the ocean (that is, the long-term market valuation of certain fundamentals) to measure the *current* height of the tides (the current market valuation of the same fundamentals).

Summary

The existence of Noise Traders is a centerpiece of the noise trader model (NTM). In simple terms, investor sentiment (or noise trader demand) may be defined as any investor demand or price pressure not aligned with news about fundamentals. In the NTM, investor sentiment can

---

[14]This approach is analogous to fixed income arbitrageurs who routinely compare the warranted yield on bonds to the actual yield at a given point in time to uncover profit opportunities. Bhojraj and Lee [2002] demonstrate how warranted multiples can help identify peer firms. In practice, many quantitative asset managers already implicitly make such an adjustment when they neutralize their value signals to industry, size, and other firm characteristics that consistently explain firms' implied cost of capital.

cause prices to move away from fundamental value. Investor sentiment could be driven either by differential liquidity needs, preferences, or information sets; or alternatively by behaviorally induced biases in the assessment of currently available information.

Although the idea that noise traders can affect prices is often identified with the behavioral finance literature, it is not unique to this literature. Noise traders were an integral part of the noisy rational expectation models and Kyle's [1985] models in market microstructure. In these models, noise traders trade for exogenous liquidity reasons. What is unique about the behavioral models is that these traders are assumed to trade not only for liquidity reasons, but also because they also tend to misperceive the present value of firms' future fundamentals.

In the NTM, the demand of noise traders affects prices in at least three important ways. First, the synchronized activities of noise traders is the reason prices deviate away from fundamentals, thus their collective actions are the primary source of the market mispricing in equilibrium. At the same time, as Black [1986] observed, it is noise trader demand that provides the opportunity for smart money to earn a higher return by investing in information acquisition and analysis. Therefore, while noise traders *cause* mispricing, they are also the ultimate source of funding for the arbitrageurs (smart money).

Second, noise trading is a key source of market risk, which is priced in equilibrium. The fact that the actions of these noise traders are difficult to predict introduces an additional element of risk to all market participants. This is seen as the risk premium is associated with arbitrage costs (the $\square$ parameter), which appears in the denominator of the market clearing price. Finally, the severity of the effect of noise trading is also related to the cost of arbitrage. Specifically, the magnitude of the mispricing is a function of how costly it is for smart money to eliminate the activities of the noise traders.[15]

This noise trader demand might come from exogenous liquidity shocks that are non-fundamental in origin. In the ensuing years,

---

[15] For simplicity, the model assumes that noise trader demand is exogenous. In reality, the nature and extent of expected noise trader demand (the $E_t(Y_{(t+i)})$ term) is unlikely to be independent from the size of the risk premium smart money demands for holding the risky asset (the $\square$ term).

an extensive literature on investor sentiment and noise trading has emerged, with implications for empirical asset-pricing, corporate finance, financial accounting, and macroeconomics. More complex and sophisticated models have been developed that attempt to provide more structure on the dynamics of noise trading and under various forms of constrained arbitrage. However, simple as it may seem, the basic framework outline in Shiller's [1984] study has survived largely intact in the literature today.

3

Noise Trading and Investor Sentiment

Investor sentiment refers to "non-fundamental" demand, that is, net demand for an asset (either to purchase or sell) that is not based on an optimal forecast of its fundamental value. Non-fundamental demand plays an important role in real-world markets, as well as in analytical models involving noise traders. On the one hand, it is a source of mispricing (and thus opportunity) for investors who expend resources on fundamental analysis in hopes of profiting from short-term price dislocations. On the other hand, it is also a source of risk, as fluctuating investor sentiment imposes a cost on all investors.

Perhaps no topic in behavioral finance has seen more recent progress than investor sentiment. Over the past few decades the literature has moved from a general debate over the existence of investor sentiment to much more focused studies that: (a) measure non-fundamental demand using novel data sources, (b) trace the origins of sentiment-based trading for specific groups of investors, and (c) assess the economic consequences of investor sentiment for asset prices and corporate decisions.

Classic references on investor sentiment include Shiller [1984], DeLong et al. [1990a], Lee et al. [1991], and Baker and Wurgler [2006, 2007]. Although terminologies differ, all these studies feature noise traders with erroneous stochastic beliefs that collectively affect prices. Another feature of these studies is their focus on "market-wide sentiment". In these studies, noise trader risk is systemic and pervasive, affecting many assets at the same time. However, as we discuss below, the concept of non-fundamental demand is much broader. Investor sentiment does not manifest itself only at the level of market aggregates. Non-fundamental demand is also important in the relative pricing of individual securities, as well as in sub-categories of securities, such as industries, geographical regions, and investment styles.

In this section, we outline the evolution of academic thinking related to investor sentiment. Our coverage will proceed in roughly chronological order. During the 1970s and 1980s, the focus in this field was on documenting/proving the existence of investor sentiment. The central issue is whether anything, apart from fundamental news, can move market prices. Over time, an accumulation of evidence pointed toward multiple liquidity and/or behavioral based-reasons for prices to move even absent fundamental news.

From the mid-1980s to the end of the last millennium, empirical researchers developed various measures of investor sentiment. A number of theoretical models emerged that propose sentiment-based explanations for asset-pricing regularities.[1] In corporate finance, researchers began to examine the conjecture that investor sentiment can impact real economic decisions by managers (this is sometimes referred to as the "catering hypothesis").[2] At the same time, the asset-pricing literature began to bifurcate, with one branch (mostly in finance) focused primarily on market-wide sentiment and another branch (mostly in accounting) focused on firm-specific sentiment and characteristic-based mispricing indicators.

---

[1] A large number of behavioral models have appeared in recent years, featuring noise traders and constrained arbitrageurs. This large literature is mostly beyond the scope of our discussion here (see Barberis and Thaler, 2002, Barberis, 2013 for good summaries), although we do discuss the subset of models featuring agents with "limited attention" or "incomplete information".

[2] The literature on behavioral corporate finance has also become vast. Because of its tangential relationship with the market efficiency literature, we only provide cursory coverage in this section. Interested readers are referred to a recent survey by Baker and Wurgler [2012].

From 2000 onwards, the pace of innovation accelerated. Recent empirical studies have linked market-wide sentiment to a host of other phenomena, such as weather and mood indicators, seasonal return patterns, capital flows, corporate stock issuances, aggregate investments, and liquidity constraints. Firm-level sentiment has been associated with sluggish price adjustment to earnings news, corporate disclosures, earnings quality metrics, cross-sectional differences in firms' investment and financing decisions, analyst forecast errors, mutual fund trades, and many other variables.

Collectively, this research has provided a wealth of new insights into the economic and psychological roots of investor sentiment, and its relation to several closely-related concepts, such as information uncertainty, limited attention, and arbitrage costs. The emerging portrait is that of a market buffeted by many types of non-fundamental demand, some from identifiable investor "clienteles" (such as retail investors or mutual funds), each exerting its influence on asset prices. Whenever the supply of rational money is insufficient to offset this sentiment-driven demand, prices are destabilized and we observe subsequent return reversals.

Propelled by a surge of new ideas, new evidence, and new data sources, this research is re-shaping our understanding of the price discovery process. Judging from its page-share in recent issues of top-tier journals, investor sentiment research has come of age. In our minds, this is a particularly fertile area of current research.

3.1 Investor sentiment and arbitrage costs

It is useful from the outset to acknowledge the inextricable link between investor sentiment and arbitrage costs (or "market frictions", as some prefer to call it). These two topics overlap and cannot be fully separated from each other. In the absence of arbitrage costs, investor sentiment would have no effect on price. At the same time, issues such as asset complexity, investor attention, and information uncertainty almost certainly have implications for both the degree of noise trading (investor sentiment) and the costs associated with exploiting the mispricing (arbitrage costs).

In the next section, we will examine the topic of market frictions. For now, it suffices to note that frictions alone do not explain mispricing. While studies of market frictions might shed light on why prices fail to correct immediately, they offer no insights into why prices stray from value in the first place. To understand the origins of mispricing, we need either a behavioral-based theory of systematic mistakes or some other explanation for correlated directional trading of a non-fundamental nature.

To be sure, decision biases identified in the psychology literature could indeed be the primary reason we observe investor sentiment. An extensive literature in psychology and experimental economics show that human subjects do not function as perfect Bayesians. In revising probabilities, human beings overweight factors such as signal saliency and the ease with which similar events are recalled, and underweight indicators of statistical reliability (see, for example, Griffin and Tversky [1992]). The quality of human judgement under uncertainty is further affected by task complexity, framing, moods and feelings, as well as a host of issues associated with self-esteem preservation (see, for example, Hirshleifer [2001], Barberis and Thaler [2002], Shiller [1999], and Hirshleifer [2015]).

However, for purposes of this discussion, it is useful to think more broadly about the origins of non-fundamental demand. Such demand could, for example, also arise from a common liquidity shock. When an asset manager is unwinding a large portfolio, her actions will exert downward price pressure on the stocks in the portfolio. Similarly, a group of traders could simultaneously buy or sell a particular asset for funding-related reasons. In each case the underlying asset will experience non-fundamental price pressure, even though the demand may not be traceable to a specific behavioral bias.

From the perspective of a long-term investor trading on fundamentals, both types of price pressure present an opportunity to benefit from costly informational arbitrage. At the same time, both also represent a source of non-fundamental risk to rational arbitrageurs facing capital constraints [DeLong et al., 1990a, Shleifer and Vishny, 1997]. Because both *behavioral biases* and *liquidity shocks* can give rise to non-fundamental demand, for purposes of this discussion, both are viewed as a potential source of investor sentiment.

In sum, studies of market frictions have an important role to play in advancing our understanding of price discovery. However, frictions alone cannot explain the tendency for prices to stray from value. To understand the latter, we need to examine either behavioral biases (the causes of the correlated mistakes), or common liquidity shocks (the sources of correlated liquidity demand across traders). That is, the domain of the investor sentiment literature covered in this section.

3.2 What moves stock prices?

What evidence do we have that stock prices move for non-fundamental reasons? Event studies show that stock prices react immediately to announcements about company earnings, dividend changes, sales projections, corporate actions, macroeconomic news, regulatory policies, and a host of other news items that could plausibly affect firm fundamentals. This evidence is often interpreted as support for market efficiency. However, as Cutler et al. [1989] observed, the stronger claim that market prices *only* respond to fundamental news is much more difficult to substantiate.

In fact, when it comes to explaining price movements with fundamentals, extensive efforts by many researchers have yielded singularly modest results. For example, accounting researchers have known for some time now that the overall fit of the earnings–returns regression is poor, with earnings explaining around 10% of the variation in annual cross-sectional returns [Lev, 1989, Easton and Harris, 1991]. Incorporating a broader set of explanatory variables nominated by valuation theory, such as changes in profitability, growth opportunities, and discount rates, can bring the explanatory power up to around 20% [Chen and Zhang, 2007]. Further including revisions of analyst expectations about future earnings elevates the explanatory power to around 30% [Liu and Thomas, 2000, Copeland et al., 2004]. In other words, armed with the latest valuation theory and our best empirical proxies for firm-level fundamental news, accounting researchers have only been able to explain a fraction (that is, around 30%) of the cross-sectional variation in annual returns. Most of the variation in cross-sectional returns (that is, 70%) remains a mystery.

News from the empirical asset-pricing literature is no better. A central and consistent result from this research is that the best explanatory variable for a firm's returns is the contemporaneous returns of other firms, and even then the explanatory power is surprisingly low [Roll, 1988]. Macroeconomic variables that *should* affect aggregate market returns (such as "innovations" in industrial production, risk premia on bonds, the term structure of interest rates, and expected inflation) provide little explanatory power for realized returns [Chen et al., 1986, Cutler et al., 1989].

Even with the most powerful econometric models, under the most generous definitions of what constitutes fundamental news, researchers have only been able to explain a fraction of the observed volatility in prices. For example, in Cutler et al. [1989], annual aggregate market returns are regressed against a large array of fundamental metrics in a VAR system of equations. Although the authors included a host of proxies for fundamental news from past, current, as well as future time periods, their models explained less than half of the observed variance in market returns. Conversely, they find that the most dramatic market moves often occurred in the absence of any fundamental news. This difficulty in explaining returns with fundamentals is not confined to equity markets. Similar findings are reported for foreign exchange markets [Frankel and Meese, 1987], bond markets [Shiller, 1979], and the market for orange juice futures [Roll, 1984].

In related work, Shiller [1981a,b] and LeRoy and Porter [1981] used a variance bound test to argue that the realized volatility of the stock market is far greater than could be justified by changes in dividends. This result was initially challenged on statistical grounds [Kleidon, 1986, Marsh and Merton, 1986], but has been largely upheld upon further review [Kleidon, 1988, Shiller, 1988, West, 1988, Engel, 2005]. By and large, the volatility of market returns relative to changes in expected cash flows remains a troubling phenomenon for empirical asset-pricing models.

Inter-temporal variations in discount rates have been advanced as the main reason why returns appear more volatile than expected dividends. If we take the market implied cost-of-capital (the internal rate-of-return implied by the current market price and expected dividends) as the "correct" rate for discounting future cash flows, then market price would equal fundamental value by tautology. However, the problem then becomes one of explaining the large inter-temporal variations in the discount rate that would be needed to rationalize price and value at each point in time (see, for example, Campbell and Shiller [1988a], Elton [1999], Pastor and Stambaugh [1999], and Cochrane [2011]).

In sum, when compared to sensible value estimates, asset prices in financial markets still seem unsettlingly volatile. At the market-level, we continue to observe extended periods of rapid expansion ("booms") as well as painful contraction ("busts"). At the firm-level, the dispersion in cross-sectional returns has been equally difficult to reconcile with observable changes in firm fundamentals. Although the reasons for these price gyrations are not fully understood, increasingly economists are looking beyond traditional valuation models for the answers.

3.3 The quest for sentiment — early work

What else, besides fundamental news, might cause prices to move? As it turns out, the task of documenting the origin and existence of investor sentiment is far from straightforward. To demonstrate the relevance of non-fundamental demand (that is, demand that is not part of rational pricing of expected cash flows) researchers need to distinguish it from demand of a fundamental nature. This is difficult because true intrinsic value is, unfortunately, not observable.

Some of the early evidence for the existence of investor sentiment was quite circumstantial. For example, French and Roll [1986] examine a period when the U.S. market is closed on Wednesdays. They use these closures to show that variation in stock returns is larger when the stock market is open than when it is closed, even during periods of similar information release about market fundamentals. This suggests that trading itself begets volatility in the absence of news, but it does not identify the source of the additional volatility.

In related research, Shleifer [1986] reports that the inclusion of a stock in the S&P500 Index is associated with a price increase of 2 to 3%. Index inclusion presumably provides no new information about firms' fundamental value, so the price increase is consistent with demand curves for stocks sloping downward. This evidence suggests that a firm's share price is influenced by net demand for the stock, and is not solely a forecast of the firm's expected future cash flows. On the other hand, Denis et al. [2003] find that newly added firms experience significant increases in analysts' earnings forecasts and improvements in realized earnings, suggesting that S&P Index inclusion may not be an information-free event after all. More recently, Barberis et al. [2004] find that after its addition to the index, a stock's correlation (beta) with the S&P also increases, once again suggesting that non-fundamental demand matters. Finally, Boyer [2011] finds that inclusion in a new S&P/Barra index increases a stock's co-movement with that index, even if that stock's fundamentals have not changed. Overall, this exchange illustrates the non-trivial challenges faced by researchers when attempting to document the effect of investor sentiment on prices.

Lee et al. [1991] tackled this problem by examining the pricing of closed-end mutual funds. Most mutual funds are open-ended, in the sense that the fund stands ready to accept more money at any time and will redeem shares for current stockholders at the "net asset value" (NAV) of the fund. In contrast, closed-end funds raise a certain amount of capital and issue a fixed number of shares through an IPO. The manager of the fund then invests in a portfolio of other traded securities, whose net asset value is "marked to market" on Friday's close, and reported weekly. The shares of closed-end funds are traded on organized stock markets. An investor in a closed-end fund who wants to liquidate must sell the shares at the market price. Because a fund's share price is set by supply and demand, it can diverge from the fund's net asset value.

The closed-end fund puzzle is the empirical observation that the NAV of these funds typically does not equal their stock price (SP). Most closed-end funds trade at a discount to their NAV, although sometimes they can trade at a premium. Lee et al. (1991) show that it is not unusual to observe closed-end funds trading at discounts of up to -30 to -40% relative to their NAV or premiums of $+10$ to 15% or more. This is true even for diversified funds that hold extremely liquid securities — the difference between SP and NAV is often much larger for funds that hold restricted securities or are themselves less frequently traded (on occasion, the premia on some funds have even exceeded 150%).

Lee et al. [1991] interpreted the discount on closed-end funds as an individual (or retail) investor sentiment index. In support of this view, they show that closed-end funds are primarily held by retail investors, and that the discounts of individual closed-end funds exhibit a strong co-movement. They argue that when retail investors are bullish (bearish), the SP of these funds increases (decreases) relative to their NAV, and closed-end fund discounts collectively narrow (widen). Their analyses show that other assets which are widely held by retail investors — such as shares of small firms, and particularly low-institutionally-owned stocks — also co-move with closed-end fund discounts. In addition, Lee et al. [1991] find that retail sentiment is related to the timing of IPO activities, with discounts narrowing in advance of "hot issuance" periods.

The original Lee et al. study led to a lively exchange between the authors and Chen et al. [1993a,b].[3] Whichever side one comes out on this debate, the curious pricing of closed-end funds has clearly altered many researchers' priors about the existence of investor sentiment. By any measure, closed-end funds are transparent and relatively easy-to-value entities (they are the "one-cell amoebas of accounting," where fair value accounting is applied to the entire balance sheet on a weekly basis). If the stock prices of these funds can routinely differ from their net asset values by $+10\%$ to -30%, what should our priors be about the magnitude of typical price deviations from value for much more complex firms, such as Tesla Motors or Apple Computers?

Closed-end funds are not the only example of relatively transparent price deviations from value. Froot and Dabora [1999] investigate the

---

[3]See, for example, Chopra et al. [1993a,b], Chan et al. [1990], Bodurtha et al. [1995], and Hanley et al. [1996]. Anderson and Born [2002] and Cherkes [2012] summarize this literature.

pricing "Siamese twin" companies whose stocks trade in different markets. These stocks have claims on an identical cash flow stream, yet their prices can diverge substantially (the pricing deviation ranges from −35% to +10% in the case of Royal Dutch/Shell). Analogous to Lee et al. (1991), these authors find that the relative prices of the twins co-move with the markets on which they trade most — that is, a twin's relative price rises (falls) when the market on which it is traded relatively intensively rises (falls). Examining a number of explanations for this phenomenon, they conclude that country-specific sentiment shocks and market frictions are the most likely causes of the often substantial price divergences.

In his presidential address to the AFA on the subject of "Noise", Black observed that since all estimates of value are noisy, we can never know how far away price is from value. He then famously quipped:

> However, we might define an efficient market as one in which price is within a factor of 2 of value, that is, the price is more than half of value and less than twice value. The factor of 2 is arbitrary, of course. Intuitively, though, it seems reasonable to me, in the light of sources of uncertainty about value and the strength of the forces tending to cause price to return to value. By this definition, I think almost all markets are efficient almost all the time. "Almost all" means at least 90%. [Black, 1986, p. 533].

The notion that stock prices in most markets can routinely deviate from fundamental values by a factor of 2 might have seemed preposterous to many back in 1986. Yet the evidence from closed-end funds and Siamese-twins stocks, as well as other studies discussed below, suggests Black might not be too far off after all.

3.4 Behavioral roots: The origins of investor sentiment

Noise trading is trading on noise as if it were information.
People who trade on noise are willing to trade even though

> *from an objective point of view they would be better off not
> trading. Perhaps they think the noise they are trading on
> is information. Or perhaps they just like to trade.* [Black,
> 1986, p. 531]

Why do people trade on noise? One reason is that they simply like to
do it. Economic models can accommodate this by modifying agents'
utility functions, but as Black [1986] observed, "Once we let trading
enter the utility function directly (as a way of saying that people like
to trade), it's hard to know where to stop. If anything can be in the
utility function, the notion that people act to maximize expected utility
is in danger of losing much of its content." (p. 534).

A more interesting possibility is that people actually think the noise
they are trading on is information. In other words, some traders may
have trouble deciphering the information content of incoming signals.
Note that this explanation does not require massive irrationality. With
a continuous stream of new data, it is extremely difficult, even for
sophisticated investors, to know whether a private signal is already
incorporated into price [Stein, 2009]. As a result, we may all engage in
noise trading to some extent. It is simply part of the price discovery
process.

The issue then is how we might learn to mitigate the problem —
that is, to become more aware of the circumstances under which we tend
to engage in noise trading. A logical starting point is the foundational
research on human cognition and decision making under uncertainty
carried out by behavioral economists, psychologist, sociologists, and
anthropologists.

In fact, an extensive literature in experimental economics shows
that human subjects follow certain behavioral principles when making decisions under uncertainty. Summarizing this literature, Shiller
[1999] identified 12 behavioral principles, and discusses the experimental evidence for each. Specifically, his survey covers: prospect theory,
regret and cognitive dissonance, anchoring, mental compartments, overconfidence, over- and under-reaction, representativeness heuristic, the
disjunction effect, gambling behavior and speculation, perceived irrel-
evance of history, magical thinking, quasi-magical thinking, attention

anomalies, the availability heuristic, culture and social contagion, and global culture.

Why don't people simply learn their way out of biased judgments? To some extent they do. However, many of the most persistent heuristic-based behaviors have "common roots" that are deeply ingrained in the human psyche. In a superb synopsis of the psychology literature from the perspective of a financial economist, Hirshleifer [2001] argues that these deeply rooted tendencies in human cognition are "hard-wired". The effects of these deeply rooted biases may be reduced through learning, he argues, but not fully eliminated.

As an organizing framework, Hirshleifer [2001] identifies three main categories of biases: (1) heuristic simplifications, (2) self-deceptions, and (3) emotional loss of control. These three categories are summarized in Table 3.1 and discussed below.

Heuristic simplifications are decision biases that have their root in our limited processing power. These include attention/memory/ease-of-processing effects, such as salience and availability biases, habits, and halo effects. Cognitive processing constraints also contribute to problems related to narrow framing, mental accounting, anchoring and adjustment, and regret aversion. Finally, heuristic-based thinking leads to non-Bayesian belief updating, the gambler's fallacy, and the hot-hand illusion. In short, many of the problems identified by the behavioral experimental literature seem to find their root in the coping mechanisms (decision heuristics) human beings use to deal with cognitive processing constraints.

Self-deceptions are decision biases that are rooted in our need for the preservation of self-esteem or a sense of self-worth. These include overconfidence (more so when task is challenging and feedback is noisy), the self-attribution bias (a tendency to attribute good outcomes to skill and bad one to luck), cognitive dissonance (action-induced attitude changes), the sunk cost effect, the disposition effect (slow to realize losses, too fast to sell winners), the hindsight bias, ex post rationalization ("I knew it all along"), and the confirmatory bias (searching for confirmatory rather than contradictory evidence). In short, human beings appear to have a deep-rooted obsession with self-esteem preservation which leads to sub-optimal decisions.

Table 3.1: Common Roots of Biased Judgement (based on Hirshleifer [2001]).

A. Heuristic Simplifications
Decision biases that seem rooted in our limited processing power.

A.1 Attention/Memory/Ease-of-Processing Effects
* Salience and availability (ease-of-recall affecting probability assessment)
* Habits (to cope with memory constraints and self-regulation)
* Halo effect (to simplify complex evaluations)

A.2 Narrow framing/Mental Accounting/Reference Effects
* Framing effects (analyzing problems in too isolated a fashion)
* Mental accounting; disposition effect, house money effect
* Anchoring; regret aversion; loss aversion

A.3 Representativeness Heuristic
* Law of small numbers (underweighting of base-rates)
* Gambler's fallacy; hot-hand illusion

A.4 Belief Updating: Combining Effects
* Conservatism (anchoring)
* Griffin and Tversky [1992]: strength (salience) versus weight (reliability)

B. Self-deception
Decision biases rooted in our need to preserve self-worth or a sense of self-esteem.

* Overconfidence (even more so when task is challenging and feedback is noisy)
* Self-attribution bias (taking credit for favorable outcomes but not negative ones)
* Cognitive dissonance (action-induced attitude changes)
* Sunk cost effect (be unduly influenced by past decisions and costs)

(Continued)

Table 3.1: (*Continued*).

---

* Confirmation bias (proclivity to search for confirming vs. contradictory evidence)
* Disposition effect (too slow to realize losses, too fast to sell winners)
* Hindsight bias; rationalization ("knew it all along")

C. Emotions and Self-control
Decision biases that seem rooted in problems of self-control

C.1 Distaste for Ambiguity
* The Ellsberg paradoxes [Ellsberg, 1961]
* Ambiguity aversion; the control illusion (choosing fund managers?)

C.2 Mood, Feelings, and Decisions
* For example, OSU victories and the sale of Ohio Lottery tickets
* How bodily sensations and cognitive experiences affect decision making

C.3 Time Preference and Self-control
* Inter-temporal choice; Deferring consumption involves self-control
* Sometimes discount rates seem remarkably high

Emotional loss of control gives rise to a set of decision biases rooted in lapses of self-control or self-discipline. These include the Ellsberg paradoxes [Ellsberg, 1961], ambiguity aversion, control illusion, the effect of mood and feelings on financial decisions, as well as intertemporal choices that involve deferred consumption. The idea is that rational decision making can also be sometimes influenced by our bodily sensations and cognitive experiences.

Hirshleifer [2001] argues that most of the physical and psychological factors that lead to sub-optimal decisions fall into one of these three categories. In a more recent review article, Hirshleifer [2015] further emphasizes the social aspect of human behavior. Specifically, the follow-up study highlights the effect of social interactions and contagion behavior in the propagation of individual cognitive biases. Rather than studying "behavioral finance", Hirshleifer [2015] calls for more work on "social finance".

In short, a large literature in experimental economics shows that human judgment is often affected by physical and psychological factors that lead to sub-optimal decisions. The quality of our judgement is further affected by a host of factors, including task-complexity, framing, moods and feelings, as well as issues associated with self-esteem preservation. Far from being eliminated by social interactions, these biases can often be amplified by engagements with others.

A detailed discussion of each of the phenomena discussed in the behavioral literature is beyond the scope of this monograph. Interested readers are encouraged to read the excellent overviews by Barberis and Thaler [2002], Shiller [1999], and Hirshleifer [2001, 2015]. However, be forewarned: none of these studies will provide a clean one-to-one mapping between the investor psychology literature and specific market anomalies. Rather, their goal is to simply set out the experimental evidence from psychology, sociology, and anthropology. The hope is that, thus armed, financial economists would be more attuned to, and more readily recognize, certain market phenomena as manifestations of these enduring human foibles.

Do these behavioral problems actually matter in financial markets? In the next sub-section, we survey the evidence on the existence and impact of investor sentiment.

3.5 Capital flows and stock returns

In our minds, the empirical association between capital flows and stock returns represents one of the most compelling pieces of evidence on the existence of investor sentiment. Over multiple asset classes and across many markets, investor flows are positively correlated with lagged and contemporaneous returns, and negatively correlated with subsequent returns. Time and again, the evidence shows that capital chases performance, but performance itself is not persistent. In fact, overall performance tends to reverse after periods of large capital inflows or outflows.

At the aggregate level, most of the money arrives just before markets decline, and most of the money exits just before markets rise [Ben-Rephael et al., 2012, Baker and Wurgler, 2000, Nelson, 1999, Loughran et al., 1994]. This pattern is observed in multiple equity markets around the world [Dichev, 2007, Baker et al., 2012]. The same uncannily poor timing ability is observed for investor flows in/out of individual stocks [Lee and Swaminathan, 2000, Baker and Wurgler, 2002], as well as for flows in/out of professionally managed investment vehicles, such as mutual funds and hedge funds [Fung et al., 2008, Dichev and Yu, 2011]. In all these instances, higher (lower) capital flows portend lower (higher) future returns. We survey the evidence below and discuss its implications.

Dichev [2007] makes a distinction between the return to a security and the return to an investor. The first is the passive "buy-and-hold" returns for holding the security; the second is a "dollar-weighted" return, based on total capital deployed at each point in time. In other words, the actual historical returns to investors are determined not only by the returns on the securities they hold but also by the timing and magnitude of their capital flows into and out of these securities. Dichev [2007] shows that in most of the developed markets, investors' actual historical returns are much lower than the buy-and-hold returns. For the NYSE/AMEX from 1926 to 2002, the return differential is 1.3% per year. For 19 other major international stock markets from 1973 to 2004, the return differential is 1.5% per year. For the NASDAQ from 1973 to 2002, it is a whopping 5.3% per year. These highly statistically significant differences arise because in all these markets, higher capital inflows (outflows) portend lower (higher) future returns.[4]

---

[4]More recently, Ben-Rephael et al. [BWK, 2012] examine the relation between capital flows and market-wide returns using monthly data of flows to/from aggregate U.S. mutual funds. Specifically, they find a positive contemporaneous relation between aggregate stock market returns and the net monthly capital flow from

In response to the capricious demand from noise traders, one might expect corporate managers to issue more equity or initiate more IPOs during market run-ups. Indeed this is what we observe during high sentiment periods [Baker and Wurgler, 2000, Nelson, 1999, Loughran et al., 1994]. Baker and Wurgler [2000], in particular, show that the share of equity issue in total new issuances (debt plus equity) is among the strongest predictors of U.S. stock market returns between 1928 and 1997. Consistent with the investor sentiment explanation, periods with high (low) equity issuance are followed by low (high) market returns.

This corporate response to investor sentiment is in essence a directional bet against the prevailing market sentiment. Corporate managers expand the supply of shares in response to perceived excess demand. If a sufficient supply of new shares appears quickly enough, this market-wide sentiment would have no appreciable effect on current prices. The fact that capital flows predict future market returns suggests that this supply of new shares is not always sufficient or readily available.

The evidence from the asset management industry is even more compelling. Flows into and out of mutual funds are strongly related to lagged measures of fund performance [Chevalier and Ellison, 1997, Sirri and Tufano, 1998]. Yet the evidence suggests that there is virtually little or no persistence in fund performance [Carhart, 1997]. In fact, the timing and magnitude of capital flows into and out of individual hedge funds has an uncanny ability to predict future fund returns. Funds that experience greater inflows subsequently underperform, while funds with greater outflows subsequently outperform [Fung et al., 2008].

Dichev and Yu [DY, 2011] report similar findings from capital flows into/out of hedge funds. Applying the method used in Dichev [2007], DY report that the annualized dollar-weighted returns to hedge fund investors are 3% to 7% lower than the corresponding buy-and-hold returns earned by the hedge fund. The entire return differential is attributable to the timing and magnitude of investor flows. Once again,

---

bond funds into equity funds. BWK show that 85% of this contemporaneous relation is reversed within four months, and 100% is reversed in 10 months. Once again, these findings are consistent with hot money chasing lagged performance, leading to subsequent price reversals. Consistent with this explanation, BWK nominate their fund-flow variable as an improved measure of investor sentiment.

we see that capital chases performance, but performance itself is not persistent. In fact, overall fund performance tends to reverse after periods of large capital inflows or outflows.[5]

It is more difficult to measure capital flows into and out of individual stocks, but what evidence we have dovetails nicely with the findings above. Both Baker and Wurgler [2002] and Dong et al. [2012] find that firms are more likely to issue (repurchase) equity when their market values are high (low) relative to fundamental value estimates — in short, firms time issuances so as to exploit apparent mispricings relative to fundamentals. Consistent with this explanation, firms that issue shares through IPOs [Ritter, 1991, Brav and Gompers, 1997] and secondary stock offerings [Loughran and Ritter, 1995, Spiess and Affleck-Graves, 1995] experience lower future returns. Conversely, firms repurchasing their shares earn higher future returns [Ikenberry et al., 1995, Peyer and Vermaelen, 2009]. The evidence is similar when using a net financing metric from the financial statements that combine debt and equity financing [Bradshaw et al., 2006], and within international studies using data from 41 other countries [McLean et al., 2009].

In all these instances, the timing of investor flows into or out of a stock is negatively correlated with its future returns. Collectively, investors seem to be going into these stocks at precisely the wrong times. In each case, the directional flow of the capital seems to run contrary to valuation metrics. Investors seem unduly influenced by recent past performance and pay insufficient attention to fundamental indicators of long-term value.

For example, analyzing the IPOs issued between 1980 and 1997, Purnanandam and Swaminathan [2004] that they are overvalued by 14% to 50% depending on peer-matching criteria. The authors conclude that IPO investors were misled by optimistic growth forecasts and paid

---

[5]Note that the lack of persistence in manager performance need not imply that these managers do not have differential ability. It could be that the more skillful managers attract increasingly large amounts of capital, and that the larger capital base then serves as a drag on future performance. For example, in Berk and Green [2004], markets learn about managers with heterogeneous skill levels over time. This learning model would seem to be less relevant, however, in the case of market-wide fund flows and returns. See Christoffersen et al. [2014] for an excellent survey of the literature on investor flows.

insufficient attention to profitability in valuing IPOs. Likewise, Arif and Lee [2015] find that during periods of heavy (light) aggregate corporate investments, analysts' forecasts of future macroeconomic and firm-specific growth are too optimistic (pessimistic).[6]

In sum, although the causes and consequences of investor flows is an on-going area of research (see Christoffersen et al. [2014] for an excellent summary), some stylized facts are clear. Flows of investment capital are highly sensitive to past performance and do not seem to pay sufficient attention to fundamentals. These flows are a source of opportunity for fundamental investors and corporate managers, but they also represent a source of risk.

3.6 Investor clienteles and systemic noise

To be price relevant, the capricious (non-fundamental) outlooks/moods of the individuals need to be directionally correlated. Do we have any direct evidence that noise trading is correlated across investor clienteles? Does this type of noise trading have significant pricing implications? As it turns out, a large body of evidence now points to an affirmative answer to both questions.

3.6.1 Retail traders

Kumar and Lee [2006] examine more than 1.85 million investor transactions obtained from a large U.S. retail brokerage house. They find that these trades are systematically correlated — that is, individuals buy (or sell) stocks in concert. This common directional component in retail trades is not explained by overall market returns or fundamental factors (both macro and firm-specific). More importantly, they find that systematic retail trading explains return co-movements for stocks

---

[6]We have focused on the net issuance anomalies because they are a clear example of investor flows going into or out of a specific stock. However, the idea of firm-specific sentiment showing up in investor flows is much more pervasive. For example, Lee and Swaminathan [2000] find that high-volume stocks earn lower future returns, and attribute their findings to a glamour/value effect whereby the price of high-volume (low-volume) stocks reflect excessive investor optimism (pessimism).

with high retail concentration (that is, small-cap, value, lower institutional ownership, and lower-priced stocks), especially if these stocks are also hard to arbitrage. They conclude retail trades have a common non-fundamental directional component which impacts stock returns.[7]

Just how much do individual investors lose by trading? Barber et al. [2009a] examine this question using a remarkable data set from the Taiwan Stock Exchange which contains a complete trading history of all investors. This data allow the authors to identify trades made by individuals and by four different categories of institutions (corporations, dealers, foreigners, and mutual funds). Their results show that individuals collectively suffer an annual performance penalty of 3.8%, which is equivalent to 2.2% of Taiwan's GDP. Institutions enjoy an annual performance boost of 1.5%, with foreign institution garnering nearly half of the profits. Over their study period (1995–1999) Taiwan was the world's 12th largest financial market. Like the other studies on retail trading, this study shows that retail activity is directionally correlated across individual traders. Moreover, it is price destabilizing in the short-run, resulting in net losses for retail investors of a large economic magnitude.

Multiple other studies have examined the performance of retail investors. By and large, the news is not good (at least for the retail investors). As a group, these traders tend to move in concert, and their trading generally result in net losses (see Barber and Odean, 2015 for summary). A few studies report persistent trading skill in certain subsets of retail investors,[8] but the broad stylized fact is that retail trading is price destabilizing, and that retail traders tend to lose to institutional investors. These findings point to correlated trading

---

[7] For further evidence of small trader herding and price destabilization, see Barber et al. [BOZ, 2009b]. Using transaction data and identifying buyer- or seller-initiated trades, BOZ show that daily small-trade imbalance reliably predicts returns — positively over shorter (weekly) horizons, and negatively over longer (12-month) horizons. This evidence suggests that correlated retail trading tends to "push" price too far in the short-run, and that returns subsequently reverse in the long-run.

[8] For example, Ivkovic and Weisbenner [2005] find that the local holdings of individual investors perform particularly well, and Ivkovic et al. [2008] report that individuals with concentrated portfolios also perform well. Similarly, Coval et al. [2005] find that some individual investors are systematically better than others.

across individuals (non-professionals) as at least part of what constitutes investor sentiment.[9]

3.6.2 Mutual fund flows

Retail investors are not the only ones who engage in noise trading. A growing body of work finds that Mutual funds (MFs), which collectively control over 40% of the shares in U.S. equity markets, are also responsible for systemic price-destabilizing trades.

In a seminal study, Coval and Stafford [2007] examine institutional price pressure caused by mutual fund transactions that can be predicted in advance. Using MF holdings as reported in quarterly 13-F filings between 1980 and 2004, they show that MFs experiencing large outflows tend to decrease existing positions, which creates price pressure on the securities held in common by distressed funds. At the same time, funds experiencing large inflows tend to expand existing positions, thus creating positive price pressure in overlapping holdings.

Two other related studies by Frazzini and Lamont [2008] and Lou [2012] document a similar phenomenon using a different construction of the stock-specific MF flow variable. Both studies show that these price effects are relatively long-lived, lasting around two quarters and taking several more quarters (or, in the case of Lou, even years) to reverse. In each case, "popular" stocks, as evidenced by MF holdings, experience upward price moves in the short-run, followed by subsequent price reversals over longer horizons. In both studies, the flow-induced return patterns are statistically and economically significant.

Why don't smart money investors trade against these predictable MF flows? In fact, it appears that some do. Shive and Yun [2013] identify a subset of 13-F filers that are likely to be hedge funds, and show that some of these funds profit from trading against the predictable, flow-induced trades of mutual funds. Specifically they find a

---

[9]The literature on retail investor behavior is large, and we have selectively focused only on the studies that are most germane to the market pricing and investor sentiment topics at hand. The broader literature documents many behavioral biases among retail investors, such as overconfidence, the disposition effect, overly aggressive trading, and limited attention. Interested readers are referred to Barber and Odean [2015].

one standard deviation increase in trading against predictable MF flows is associated with a 0.9% higher annualized four-factor alpha for the hedge fund. This evidence shows that at least some hedges do trade in response to predictable MF flows. The fact that aggregate MF flows still portend lower returns suggests that the aggregate hedge fund trades are not enough to fully offset the price impact of MF flows.

Arif et al. [ABL, 2015] provide similar evidence at higher frequencies. Aggregating MF trades obtained from a large trading-cost consultant, ABL construct a daily directional measure of MF flows (aggregate MF buys — aggregate MF sells). They find that aggregated MF flows are strongly price destabilizing — stocks that are bought (sold) by MFs experience upward (downward) price pressure, leading to price continuation over the next week and subsequent price reversals lasting several months. In addition, ABL show that short-sellers (SS) profit from these MF trades by increasing their short-sales when MFs are buying and decreasing them when MFs are selling. The negative correlation between MF and SS results in a substantial "wealth transfer" from MFs to SSs.

Akbas et al. [2015] also find that MF flows are price destabilizing, and that hedge funds profit from these flows. Using quarterly mutual fund flows as a proxy for dumb money, and hedge fund flows as a proxy for smart money, these authors show that MF flows exacerbate well-known stock return anomalies (such as asset growth, accruals, and momentum), while hedge fund flows attenuate these anomalies.

Why do the mutual funds get things so wrong? Brown, Wei, and Wermers [BWW, 2014] shed some light on this issue. They report that MFs respond to sell-side stock recommendations. Specifically, MFs "herd" by buying (selling) stocks that have been upgraded (downgraded). As a result, the stocks that have been upgraded (downgraded) by analysts experience a same-quarter upward (downward) price move, followed by a sharp subsequent price reversal. The authors link the magnitude of this effect to measures that proxy for fund managers' career concerns. Evidently MF managers act upon analyst stock recommendations in part to protect themselves from being accused of violating the prudent man rule.

In sum, a growing literature shows that aggregate MF trading is price destabilizing. We now have substantial evidence that MF trades produce short-term price moves, which are reversed in the future [Puckett and Yan, 2013, Brown et al., 2013, Arif et al., 2015, Lou, 2012 and Lee 2015; Lou, 2012]. Some hedge funds and short-sellers seem to trade against this non-fundamental demand, but their trading is insufficient to fully eliminate the effect.[10]

3.6.3 Other investor clienteles

It would be tempting to conclude that retail investors and mutual fund managers are the primary or even the sole culprits behind price-destabilizing trades, with more sophisticated investors, such as hedge funds, always serving as corrective forces. Unfortunately neither theory nor evidence supports such a simple dichotomy.

Theory suggests that rational arbitrageurs can also engage in price-destabilizing trades. This would occur when they expects price to further deviate from fundamental value. Hart and Kreps [1986] show that even when all agents are rational and have identical priors, speculative activity does not always "stabilize" prices. Similarly, DeLong et al. [1990b] show that when noise traders follow positive-feedback strategies — buy when prices rise and sell when prices fall — rational investors may in fact prefer to ride rather than trade against the bubbles.

Consistent with these predictions, Brunnermeier and Nagel [2004] show that some hedge funds experienced large losses and net redemptions while betting against the technology bubble in the late 1990s. As the extent of mispricing deepened, some of these funds were forced to close before the bubble's collapse in 2001. The authors find that some other hedge funds did not exert a correcting force on stock prices, and

---

[10]An unresolved issue is whether mutual fund managers are hapless victims of retail investor sentiment, or whether their actions contribute to their own demise. Clearly some MF under-performance is due to flow-induced trading attributable to retail sentiment. However, MF herding might also be due to over-reliance on a common investment signal [Brown et al., 2013] or overly-rigid daily trading patterns Arif et al. [2015]. This would appear to be an interesting topic for future research.

instead invested heavily in overpriced technology stocks. The popularity of momentum-based strategies among active fund managers suggests that this type of behaviour is far from unusual [Daniel et al., 1997, Asness et al., 2014].

In addition, even hedge funds fall prey to systematic mistakes. For example, Mitchell et al. [2002] find that the professional investors trading around merger announcements engage in "herding" behavior. They estimate that nearly half of the negative announcement period stock price reaction for acquirers in stock-financed mergers reflects downward price pressure caused by merger arbitrage short-selling. In this instance, the short-sellers are engaging in an over-crowded trade, which causes them to lose money ex post. Thus even sophisticated short-selling merger arbitrageurs can destabilize prices to their own detriment.

In sum, the evidence shows that retail investors, mutual funds, and hedge funds all at times contribute to investor sentiment. These suboptimal trading patterns speak more to the difficulty of calibrating one's information than to massive irrationality. It is a challenge, even for sophisticated investors, to know whether his/her private signal is already incorporated into price [Stein, 2009]. In a noisy market, we are all noise traders.

3.7   Measuring investor sentiment

By the middle of the first decade in the new millennium, a significant effort was underway to develop useful sentiment measures. As Baker and Wurgler observed in their summary article on this subject:

> Now, the question is no longer, as it was a few decades ago,
> whether investor sentiment affects stock prices, but rather
> how to measure investor sentiment and quantify its effects.
> [Baker and Wurgler, 2007, p. 130]

In the same article, Baker and Wurgler provide a useful discussion of generic issues involved in measuring investor sentiment:

> An exogenous shock in investor sentiment can lead to a
> chain of events, and the shock itself could in principle be

> observed at any and every part of this chain. For example,
> it might show up first in investor beliefs, which could be
> surveyed. These beliefs might then translate to observable
> patterns of securities trades, which are recorded. Limited
> arbitrage implies that these demand pressures might cause
> some mispricing, which might be observed using bench-
> marks for fundamental value like the book-to-market ratio.
> These mispricings might engender an informed response by
> insiders, such as corporate executives, who may have both
> the superior information and the incentive to take advan-
> tage of it, and the patterns of firms choosing to adjust their
> balance of equity or debt could be observed. [Baker and
> Wurgler, 2007, p. 135]

The four key elements discussed above are: *belief revisions* (measured
by surveys on such matters as consumer confidence), *trading decisions*
(measured by investor fund flows or aggregate trading volume), *price
dislocations* (measured by comparing price to estimates of fundamental
value, or perhaps the pricing of IPOs), and *smart money responses*
(measured by corporate actions or insider trades).

Each of these four elements finds representation in the literature.
First, investor sentiment has been gauged through different *surveys* of
household or corporate manager beliefs [Lemmon and Portniaguina,
2006, Ho and Hung, 2009, Lamont, 2000]. Second, several measures of
investor fund *flows* have been developed that seem to capture market-
wide sentiment [Nelson, 1999, Dichev, 2007, Ben-Rephael et al., 2012].
Third, various valuation-based *market-multiples* have a demonstrated
ability to predict market-wide returns (see, for example, Campbell and
Shiller [1988b], Kothari and Shanken [1997] and Lee et al. [1999]).
Finally, *corporate actions* in response to equity market conditions,
such as the amount of equity-versus-debt financing [Baker and Wurgler, 2000] and the aggregate level of corporate investments [Arif and
Lee, 2015] also seem to reflect some aspects of fluctuating investor sentiment.

Consolidating these ideas, Baker and Wurgler [BW, 2006, 2007]
develop a composite index of market-wide sentiment consisting of six

underlying proxies: the closed-end fund discount, NYSE share turnover, the number and average first-day returns on IPOs, the equity share in new issues, and the dividend premium. They regress each proxy on a number of business cycle variables, and extract the first principal component of the six residual time-series. They find that the resulting sentiment index roughly lines up with anecdotal accounts of fluctuations in market sentiment.

BW then examine the implications of this sentiment measure for *cross-sectional* asset-pricing. Following the noise trader framework [Shiller, 1984, DeLong et al., 1990a], they hypothesize that the sensitivity of each firm's returns to the sentiment factor is a function of arbitrage costs, with more-difficult-to-arbitrage firms having higher "sentiment betas." Consistent with this hypothesis, they find a striking "see-saw" effect in cross-sectional returns whereby returns of hard-to-arbitrage (easy-to-arbitrage) firms have positive (negative) loadings on market sentiment. Baker et al. [BWY, 2012] construct sentiment indices for five other developed countries (Canada, Japan, Germany, France, and the United Kingdom), and find a similar "sentiment see-saw" effect there.

A recent study by Huang et al. [HJTU 2015] present a useful econometric refinement to the original BW index. Using a Partial Least-Squares method to aggregate the six sentiment proxies (instead of the Principle Component approach in the original BW studies), HJTU develop a new index that more fully eliminates the common noise component in the underlying proxies. Their tests show that this better-aligned sentiment index has a much stronger ability to predict aggregate stock market returns. The HJTU sentiment index also has predictive power for cross-sectional returns sorted by industry, size, value, and momentum.

Arif and Lee [AL, 2015] suggest a further refinement to the market-wide sentiment measure. Consistent with the existence of sentiment-driven business cycles, AL show that aggregate corporate investments peak during periods of positive sentiment, yet these periods are followed by lower equity returns. This pattern exists in most developed countries and survives multiple controls. Higher aggregate investments also precede greater earnings disappointments, lower short-window earnings announcement returns, and lower macroeconomic growth. Dividing existing analytical models into four groups (see Appendix 2.A), AL note that it is difficult to distinguish between Group 1 and Group 2 explanations by studying stock returns in isolation. Using additional evidence from the time-series behavior of investor sentiment variables, as well as the predictability of future cash flow "shocks," AL conclude that aggregate corporate investment is an alternative, and possibly sharper, measure of market-wide sentiment.

To sum up, prior studies have measured market-wide investor sentiment using: *belief revisions* (for example, surveys), *trading decisions* (for example, investor fund flows or trading volume), *price dislocations* (for example, valuation multiples and IPO pricing), and *smart money responses* (for example, stock issuances, corporate investments, and insider trades).

3.8 Firm-level sentiment

In the cross-section, individual firms can have differing sensitivities to this market-wide sentiment (that is, each firm has its own "sentiment beta"). In Shiller [1984], for example, these "sentiment betas" are captured by □, the premium demanded by smart traders to fully eliminate the noise traders, which we loosely interpreted as "arbitrage costs". The Shiller model predicts that firms which are more costly to arbitrage will be more sensitive to movements in market-wide sentiment. Empirically, Baker and Wurgler [2006, 2007] provide support for this prediction by showing that "hard-to-arbitrage" (smaller, more volatile, and less liquid) firms are indeed more sensitive to a market-wide sentiment index.

In theory, however, non-fundamental demand is not confined to market aggregates. Investor sentiment can exist whenever noise traders with a common erroneous belief collectively affect prices. Thus we might expect to see non-fundamental demand to impact the pricing of any asset, or group of assets. Non-fundamental demand can play a role in the relative pricing of individual industries (for example, e-commerce or biotech or consumer durables), geographical regions (for example, domestic versus foreign, Asia versus Europe), or investment "styles" (for example, value versus growth, or low-volatility versus high-volatility). When certain industries, geographic regions, or investment styles become "hot", money flows in that direction, resulting in initial price escalations, followed by subsequent return reversals [Barberis and Shleifer, 2003].

Non-fundamental demand can also manifest itself in the form of firm-specific mispricing. For example, the literature on investor sentiment has examined the effect of signal saliency and statistical reliability on the proclivity of investors to over- and under-weight individual signals. Following the lead of psychologists (see, for example, Kahneman and Tversky [1974] and Griffin and Tversky [1992]), researchers have observed a broad tendency for investors to over-weight firm-level signals that are more salient or attention grabbing (see, for example, Barber and Odean [2008], Hirshleifer et al. [2009], Da et al. [2011], and Engelberg et al. [2012b]), and under-weight signals that are statistically reliable but less salient, or required more processing to be understood (see, for example, Della Vigna and Pollet [2007], Gleason and Lee [2003], Giglio and Shue [2012], Cohen and Lou [2012], Cohen et al. [2013a,b], and So [2013]). Most of these examples involve increased task complexity and/or limited investor attention, and are discussed in more detail in Section 5 on Limits to Arbitrage.

A large body of work in accounting examines market over- and under-reaction to different types of firm-specific information. Much of this evidence points to sub-optimal usage of publicly available information about the future prospects of a specific company. Thus these studies can also be viewed as ways to uncover investor sentiment, even though they do not usually bear this moniker. In the next section, we summarize this literature by placing it in a value investing framework.

3.9   Moods and emotions

Finally, we end this section by reviewing an interesting new development in the sentiment literature on investor moods and emotions. In his recent survey article, Hirshleifer [2015] noted:

> (T)he affective revolution in psychology of the 1990s, which
> elucidated the central role of feelings in decision making, has
> only partially been incorporated into behavioral finance.
> More theoretical and empirical study is needed of how feel-
> ings affect financial decisions, and the implications of this
> for prices and real outcomes. This topic includes moral atti-
> tudes that infuse decisions about borrowing/saving, bearing
> risk, and exploiting other market participants. [Hirshleifer,
> 2015, p. 43].

Hirshleifer ends by calling for a move "from behavioral finance to *social finance* (and *social economics*)." He writes: "Behavioral finance has primarily focused on individual-level biases. Social finance promises to offer equally fundamental insight, and to be a worthy descendant of behavioral finance." [Hirshleifer, 2015, p. 45].

How might we take a measure of investor moods? One approach is to conduct surveys (see, for example, Shiller [2000] and Hong et al. [2004]). Another is to identify some exogenous external influence that has a pervasive effect on many individuals at the same time. For exam-ple, Saunders [1993] and Hirshleifer and Shumway [2003] study the impact of sunshine on average stock returns; Cao and Wei [2005] exam-ine the role of temperature in eight international markets; Kamstra et al. [2003] analyze the effect of available daylight; and Yuan et al. [2006] explore lunar cycles. In all these studies, the mood indicator is an exogenous continuous variable that is unlikely to be affected market gyrations.

The sunshine effect seems particularly robust. Saunders [1993] first showed that when it is cloudy in New York City, NYSE index returns tend to be negative. The cloudiness/returns correlation is robust to various choices of stock index and regression specifications. Hirshleifer and Shumway [2003] extend the analysis to 26 stock exchanges world-wide. Their results show that morning sunshine at the country's leading stock exchange is strongly correlated with daily stock returns. Weather-based strategies can lead to modest improvements in returns even after transaction costs, but it is not a risk-free arbitrage opportunity. The evidence is consistent with sunshine affecting mood, and mood affecting prices.[11]

Another interesting line of inquiry focuses on the influence of daylight on investor sentiment and risk tolerance. Kamstra et al. [KKL, 2003] first investigated the impact of seasonal shifts in length of day on returns to stock market indices from countries at various latitudes and on both sides of the equator. Building on psychology literature that documents a strong relation between the availability of daylight on seasonal affective disorder (SAD), KKL posit that depression associated with shorter days translates into a greater degree of risk aversion. Consistent with this proposition, KKL find that equity returns are higher during the fall and winter (seasons with less daylight), and varying conditionally across the seasons by as much as 12% (annualized). The pattern shifts by six months for markets in the southern hemisphere, and higher-latitude markets show more pronounced SAD effects.

More recently, Kamstra et al. [2013] show that aggregate investor flow data from mutual funds also reveal a preference for low-risk (U.S. money market and government bond) funds in the autumn and higher-risk (equity) funds in the spring. Similar patterns are seen in fund flows in Australia, which are six months out of phase relative to Canada and the U.S. Kamstra et al. [2014] provide a good summary of the findings to date on this literature. Collectively, these seasonal asset allocation patterns provide an unusually clear view on aggregate trading behavior that seems to map well into the psychology literature.

Another set of studies focuses on the relation between sports sentiment and stock returns. As Edmans et al. [2007] observed: "the main advantage of the event approach compared to the use of a continuous variable is that the former clearly identifies a sudden change in the mood of investors, which gives a large signal-to-noise ratio in returns. The main disadvantage of the event approach is that the number of

---

[11]Novy-Marx [2014] has a more cynical interpretation of these results. He claims, facetiously, that a similar argument can be made for the predictive power of global warming, sun spots, politics, and planetary alignments.

observed signals tends to be low, which reduces statistical power."
(p. 1968).[12]

In motivating their own study, Edmans et al. [2007, p. 1969–1970]
cite a large literature in psychology that shows sports results have a
significant effect on mood:

> Wann et al. [1994] document that fans often experience
> a strong positive reaction when their team performs well
> and a corresponding negative reaction when the team per-
> forms poorly. More importantly, such reactions extend to
> increased or decreased self-esteem and to positive or neg-
> ative feelings about life in general. Hirt et al. [1992] find
> that Indiana University college students estimate their own
> performance to be significantly better after watching a
> win by their college basketball team than after watching
> a loss. Schwarz et al. [1987] document that the outcome of
> two games played by Germany in the 1982 World Cup sig-
> nificantly changed subjects' assessments of their own well-
> being and their views on national issues.

> A related study by Schweitzer et al. [1992] shows that
> assessments of both the probability of a 1990 war in Iraq
> and its potential casualties were significantly lower among
> students rooting for the winning team of a televised Amer-
> ican football game than among fans of the losing team.
> Changes in mood also affect economic behavior. Arkes et al.
> [1988] find that sales of Ohio State lottery tickets increase
> in the days after a victory by the Ohio State Univer-
> sity football team. Given the evidence that sports results
> affect subjects' optimism or pessimism about not just their

---

[12]Other studies have focused on salient events that are not sports related. For
example, Kamstra et al. [2000] use data from several countries to show that the
Friday–Monday return is significantly lower on daylight-savings weekends than on
other weekends. They attribute this finding to the disruptions in sleep patterns
associated with the change to daylight-savings time. This evidence was challenged
by Pinegar [2002], which in turn elicited a reply by Kamstra et al. [2002]. Much of
the debate focused on the role of outliers, although both sides agree on the empirical
facts.

> own abilities, but life in general, we hypothesize that they
> impact investors' views on future stock prices. [Edmans
> et al., 2007, pp. 1969–1970]

Edmans et al. [2007] use international soccer results as their primary mood variable. They find a significant market decline after soccer losses. For example, a loss in the World Cup elimination stage leads to a next-day abnormal stock return of −49 basis points, on average. This loss effect is stronger in smaller stocks and in more important games, and is robust to various perturbations in the research design. They also find a statistically significant but smaller loss effect after international cricket, rugby, and basketball games. There is no evidence of a corresponding reaction to wins in any of these sports. Interestingly, the effect is not priced into the index even when a loss is highly expected.

In sum, a small emerging set of studies have documented a seemingly robust relation between various mood indicators and stock returns. The seasonal patterns reported by KKL are particularly intriguing. As investor flow data from around the world become more widely available, we hope further light will be shed on how investor psychology affects stock returns.

Summary

In most of economics, asset prices are a function of supply and demand. Movements in prices are indicative of imbalances in aggregate supply and demand; they signal market responses to either scarcity or surplus. Most economists would not view the price increase in a Van Gough painting as a signal about its "fundamental value". And of course, most would not draw conclusions about the pricing efficiency of the market for Van Gough paintings from a change in the price of a particular piece of art.

But when it comes to publicly-traded firms, economists seem to expect more from the market price. We commonly assume that stock prices quickly reflect all "fundamental news." We expect the price discovery mechanism to quickly distinguish such news from rumors and innuendoes that contain no news. Having begun with such an assumption, researchers are often surprised when returns do not conform to any sensible measure of changes in value.

The investor sentiment literature we survey in this section is a reminder that finance is still economics. A vast body of evidence now shows that stock prices move not only because there is news about firm fundamentals; they also move because there are non-fundamental forces at work every day, leading to supply and demand imbalances that move prices.

It is only academic hubris (that is, our overconfidence in the quality of our asset-pricing models) that blinds us from this most obvious fact about markets.

Appendix 2.A

Managerial decision making when markets are noisy

The following chart [from Arif and Lee, 2015] summarizes existing models of managerial decision making in the presence of market noise. Broadly speaking, these theories can be grouped into two camps, with each camp having two sub-branches.

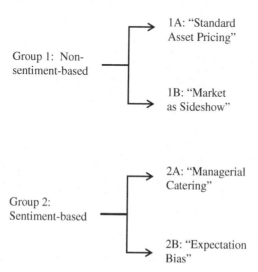

Group 1: Non-sentiment-based. Models in this group attribute the negative investment–return association to time-varying discount rates, and either assume that the stock prices are efficient (1A: the "standard asset-pricing" explanation) or that market mispricings are irrelevant to investment decisions (1B: the "market as sideshow" explanation). In these models, corporate managers behave rationally, and investor sentiment is irrelevant, either because prices are efficient [Cochrane, 1991, Carlson et al., 2006, Lyandres et al., 2008] or because managers who optimize long-term firm value rationally ignore any short-term sentiment-related fluctuations (Stein, 1996, the long-horizon case).

Group 2: Sentiment-based. Models in this group admit the possibility that investor sentiment could influence real managerial decisions. This influence occurs either because managers rationally exploit market misvaluations (2A: the "managerial catering" hypothesis) or because they are themselves caught up in the market euphoria (2B: the "expectation bias" hypothesis). The managerial catering explanation is rooted in the notion that rational managers with finite planning horizons care about temporary price dislocations (Stein, 1996, the short-horizon case). The expectation bias explanation hypothesizes that aggregate investment decisions could be influenced by the same waves of sentiment that afflict market participants.

4

Measuring Firm Value: The Role of Fundamental Analysis

This section offers an introduction to equity valuation with the goal of building a bridge between the theory and practice of value investing. We review some key insights gleaned from accounting-based valuation theory to demonstrate the inextricable conceptual link between a stock's "cheapness" and its "quality". We then use these insights as an organizing framework to discuss the essence of intelligent value investing.

We also discuss the implications of accounting-based valuation theory for market efficiency. Using examples from the asset management industry, we illustrate the key role played by equity valuation in informing investment decisions. At the same time, we show how seemingly disparate strands of empirical evidence in academic studies about the predictive power of historical accounting variables for stock returns, in fact, dovetail nicely with the investment philosophy of such legendary investors as Ben Graham, Warren Buffett, and Joel Greenblatt.

Finally, the section ends with a discussion of whether value investing will continue to be profitable in the future. In doing so, we survey potential explanations, including behavioral forces, risk, and institutional frictions, for the long-standing success of value investing discussed in the academic literature.

4.1   Overview

Value investing refers to the buying or selling of stocks on the basis of
a perceived gap between a firm's market price and its intrinsic value.
What is the intrinsic value of a firm? Here is a simple and relatively
non-controversial definition:

> *The intrinsic (equity) value of a firm is the present value of
> expected future payoffs to shareholders.*

Unlike rare art, stocks are commonly presumed to have an intrinsic
value. The intrinsic value of a Van Gogh painting is ill defined; basically,
its value is what people are willing to pay for it. But when investors
think about equity valuation, we have in mind a monetary sum that
corresponds to the present value of expected future payoffs to shareholders. Each share, after all, is simply a fractional ownership claim on
an on-going business enterprise. In contrast to other assets that carry
non-monetary benefits (such as the consumptive value of the house
we live in, or the pleasure derived from owning a painting), stocks
derive their value, by and large, from their claim to a firm's future
cash flows. Valuing these future cash flows is an integral part of value
investing because it provides investors with an independent measure of
firm value that could be used to *challenge* and perhaps *discipline* the
current market price.

Value investors buy stocks that appear to be cheap relative to their
intrinsic value, and sell (even sell short) stocks that seem expensive.
One of the most remarkable regularities in the empirical asset-pricing
literature has been the fact that value investing is consistently associated with positive abnormal returns. Both empirical academic studies
and the evidence from a host of professional asset managers seem to
confirm this. A substantial literature on finance and accounting shows
that firms trading at lower pricing multiples, with stronger balance
sheets, more sustainable cash flows, higher profitability, lower volatility, lower Beta, and lower distress risk, actually earn *higher*, not lower,
future stock returns. This pattern in cross-sectional returns, which we
refer to collectively as the "value effect", was first recognized by famed

Columbia University professor, Benjamin Graham, and documented as early as 1934. Various elements of this effect have been confirmed (and rediscovered) by a host of academic studies in the ensuing 80 years.

A common misconception among many academics and financial practitioners is that "value" is equivalent to "cheapness." Thus in many academic studies, "value stocks" are defined simply as those trading at lower market multiples (that is, lower $M/B, P/E, CF/P$, etc.).[1] This section illustrates that sensible value investing is not merely finding "cheap" stocks; it requires finding "quality" stocks (firms with strong fundamentals) trading at reasonable prices. We will provide some examples of how accounting numbers can be used, and are indeed being used, by successful professional investors to identify quality stocks. In fact, we believe that many recent results from academic research are extremely useful to value investors in their search for quality companies trading at reasonable prices.

In the remainder of this section, we revisit the theoretical underpinnings of the value effect, and summarize what is now an extensive body of evidence in support of its existence. We will get to the theory part shortly, but let us once again begin with an illustration, this time taken from the writings of Benjamin Graham.

4.2 Benjamin Graham as a quant

In one of the earliest editions of *Security Analysis*, which he co-authored with David Dodd in 1934, Graham proposed a simple stock screen. While the numbers in the screen have varied slightly across editions, the original form of this screen is preserved. Here is the original screen.[2] Any stock that possesses all 10 of the following characteristics, according to Graham, would be a worthwhile investment:

1. Earnings to price ratio that is double the AAA bond yield.

---

[1]For example, Fama and French [1992], Lakonishok et al. [1994].

[2]We are indebted to Professor Aswath Damodaran for bringing our attention to this screen. See Damodaran [2012] for an excellent historical perspective on value investing. See Cottle et al. [1988] for a more recent version of the Graham and Dodd [1934] classic.

2. PE of the stock has less than 40% of the average PE for all stocks over the last five years.

3. Dividend Yield > Two-thirds of the AAA Corporate Bond Yield.

4. Price < Two-thirds of Tangible Book Value.

5. Price < Two-thirds of Net Current Asset Value (NCAV), where net current asset value is defined as liquid current assets including cash minus current liabilities.

6. Debt–Equity Ratio (Book Value) has to be less than one.

7. Current Assets > Twice Current Liabilities.

8. Debt < Twice Net Current Assets.

9. Historical Growth in EPS (over last 10 years) > 7%.

10. No more than two years of declining earnings over the previous 10 years.

When presenting this screen, we ask students to group these 10 factors into two general categories (that is, find five factors that have more in common with each other than with the other five factors). If you stare at this screen for a few moments, you will notice that there are in fact two natural groupings. The first five factors appear to be more closely linked to each other than they are to the next five factors that follow.

   You might also recognize that the first five factors are all measures of "cheapness". The first two factors compare a company's stock price with their reported earnings, and encourage us to buy stocks whose P/E ratio is below a certain threshold. The next three compare a stock's price to its dividends, book value, and net current asset value (NCAV), respectively. Taken together, these first five factors are all instructing us to buy companies whose prices are "cheap" relative to reference measures extracted from historical financial statements.

   The next five factors differ from the first five in that they do not involve the stock price. As a group, we might refer to these five factors as measures of a firm's "quality". Notice that these factors are pure accounting constructs: financial ratios or growth rates; accounting numbers over accounting numbers. Factors 6 through 8 measure debt (or leverage), as well as short-term liquidity (or solvency). Factors 9 and 10 are measures of a company's historical earnings growth rate and the consistency of that growth. In short, Graham wants to buy firms with low leverage, high solvency, and a high and consistent rate of growth, sustained over a period of time. Quality firms, according to Ben Graham, are those with high and steady growth, low leverage, and ample liquidity.

Does this strategy work? A few years ago, a Stanford University MBA student, Becca Levin, designed a slightly updated version of this screen. Becca used the same basic formulation as Graham, but updated a couple of the constructs (substituting free-cash-flow yield, for example, in place of dividend yield; and requiring just five years of past earnings growth rather than 10 years). We recently conducted a test of this strategy using a dataset of U.S. companies over the most recent 14 years (1/2/1999 to 11/9/2013).

The Levin–Graham strategy is quite simple to implement. Specifically, we assign a +1 score if a firm meets each condition; top firms can receive a maximum score of 10, bottom firms can score as low as 0. At the beginning of each quarter, all firms are sorted into 10 portfolios according to their Levin–Graham score. We then compute the equal-weighted return for each of these 10 portfolios over the next three months. The test is performed using "as reported" Compustat data, with no survivorship or restatement issues. All variables are computed using publicly available data as of the date of portfolio formation (no "peek ahead" bias). To avoid illiquid stocks, we include only firms with a price of $3 or more. The results are reported in Figure 4.1.

This figure reports the equal-weighted return to each of these 10 portfolios over the next three months (annualized, assuming quarterly rebalancing).[3] The right-most column represents EW-returns to a

---

[3]Note that value investors can employ two related sets of strategies. The first set is comprised of fundamentally oriented value strategies such as Levin–Graham screen presented above that tend to be more focused on comparing discrepancies between price and value across firms. The second set is comprised of systematically

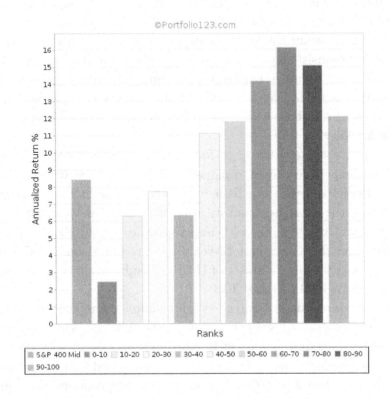

Figure 4.1: Portfolio Returns for the Levin–Graham Stock Screen Test Period 01/02/1999 to 11/13/2103.

This figure depicts the results of a backtest conducted using a sample of U.S. companies over the 01/02/1999 to 11/09/2013 time period. At the beginning of each quarter, firms are sorted into 10 portfolios according to their Levin–Graham score (based on the original Ben Graham stock screen described in the text). A firm is assign a +1 score if it meets each condition in the screen; top firms can receive a maximum score of 10, bottom firms can score as low as 0. This figure depicts the equal-weighted return to each of these 10 portfolios over the next three months (annualized, assuming quarterly rebalancing). The left-most column is the return to the S&P400 Midcap (value-weighted) index over the same time period. All variables are computed using publicly available data as of portfolio formation, and all firms with available Compustat and CRSP data and a stock price of $3 or more are included.

portfolio of firms with the highest score, and so on. The 11th (left-most) column is the return to the S&P400 Midcap (value-weighted) index over the same time period, included for comparison.

Remarkably, this 80-year-old screen continues to predict stock returns in the 21st century! In general, cheaper and higher quality stocks earn higher returns over the next three months. On an annualized basis, firms in the top two-deciles of the screen averaged around 14% per year, while firms in the bottom two-deciles averaged around 5%. The difference between these stocks is 9% per year (or equivalently, around 2.25% per quarterly rebalancing period). For comparison, the value-weighted S&P400 Midcap index returned only 8.5% over this time period. The decile results are not monotonic, but by and large, we see that cheaper and higher-quality stocks do earn higher returns even in the most recent 14-year period, in what is arguably the most efficient stock market in the world.

4.3 A bit of theory might help

What might account for this performance? Was this an unusual time period in U.S. history? To proceed further, we need to introduce a bit of valuation theory.

The Residual Income Model (RIM)

In the early to mid-1990s, Professor James Ohlson wrote a series of influential studies on equity valuation featuring what became known as the "residual income model" (RIM).[4] The RIM had its origin in the early work of financial economists.[5] Although the original model predates his work by several decades, Ohlson helped many academics

---

oriented value strategies that compare valuation metrics across related firms in the cross-section. See Lang and Lundholm [1996] for a discussion of the potential difference in the impacts these strategies on price formation.

[4]Ohlson [1990, 1991, 1995], Feltham and Ohlson [1995].

[5]See, for example, Preinreich [1938], Edwards and Bell [1961], Peasnell [1982], and Lehman [1993].

to refocus on the importance of the RIM as a means to understanding
the relation between accounting data and firm value.[6]

The most common form of the RIM in the academic literature
expresses a firm's value in terms of its current book value and future
expected abnormal accounting rates-of-returns:

$$P_t^* = B_t + \sum_{i=1}^{\infty} \frac{E_t[NI_{t+i} - (r_e^* B_{t+i-1})]}{(1+r_e)^i}$$

$$= B_t + \sum_{i=1}^{\infty} \frac{E_t[(ROE_{t+i} - r_e)^* B_{t+i-1}]}{(1+r_e)^i} \qquad (4.1)$$

where B_t = book value at time t; $E_t[.]$ = expectation based on information available at time t; NI_{t+i} = Net Income for period $t + i$; r_e = cost
of equity capital; and ROE_{t+i} = the after-tax return on book equity
for period $t + i$.[7] In this formula, the Residual Income (RI) for period t
is defined in terms of period t earnings, minus a normal rate-of-return
on the beginning capital base. Notionally: $RI_t = NI_t - (r^* B_{r-1})$. Thus,
RI reflects "value enhancing growth" in period t by capturing changes
to firms' earnings above and beyond what the firm should have earned
using its existing capital base.

An attractive aspect of the RIM is that it allows us to express firm
value (that is, the present value of a firm's future cash flows) in terms
of variables that appear in financial statements. In fact, with a sharp
pencil and some high school algebra, it is easy to show that Equation (1)
is simply a mathematical re-expression of the dividend discount model,
with the addition of the "Clean Surplus Relation".[8]

---

[6]Bernard [1995], Lundholm [1995], and Lee [1999] offer less technical discussions
on the implications of Ohlson's work. Many excellent books, including Healy and
Palepu [2012], Penman [2010, 2012], and Wahlen et al. [2010], discuss implementation details. Ohlson often underscores the fact that a RIM lacks content without
additional assumptions (for example, the "Linear Information Dynamics" assumptions in Ohlson, 1995).

[7]In this formula, the Residual Income for period t is defined in terms of period t
earnings, minus a normal rate-of-return on the beginning capital base. Notionally:
$RI_t = NI_t - (r^* B_{r-1})$. Note also that this formula refers to expected ROE, which,
strictly speaking, is not equivalent to expected earnings relative to expected book
value. The mathematic derivation calls for the latter [Penman, 1991].

[8]Clean surplus accounting requires all gains and losses affecting the starting
capital to flow through earnings. In short, any changes in the capital base must

Setting aside the details on the right hand-side of Equation (1) for a moment, notice that this equation has decomposed firm value into two components:

$$Firm\ Value_t = "Capital''_t + "PVRI''_t; \qquad (4.2)$$

where the book value at period t is "$Capital_t$", or the initial Invested Capital base, and the rest of the right-hand side is the "Present Value of Future Residual Income", hereafter referred to as "$PVRI_t$".

Equation (2) highlights the fact that Firm Value (what the firm is worth today) is always a function of two components: Invested capital (the asset base we start with today), and "Present Value of Future Residual Income" (where this asset base is going; in other words, our projection of the future value-enhancing growth in the capital base).

As it turns out, what we use as our starting capital base ($Capital_t$) really does not matter [see Penman, 1996, 1997]. In Equation (1), the current book value was used as the starting capital, but we could have chosen virtually any number as a starting capital. So long as our forecasts obey two simple rules of internal consistency, the resulting Firm Value estimate will be equivalent to the present value of a firm's future dividends.[9]

Subsequent studies featured several alternative measures of the invested capital base other than book value. For example, a firm's capitalized one-year-ahead earnings forecast, or its current year sales revenue.[10] The general RIM formula tells us that, for each invested

---

come either from earnings during the period or from net new capital flows. For example, if we define the starting capital base as the beginning-of-year book value, then the ending book value must equal the starting book value plus earnings minus net dividends: ($B_t = B_{t-1} + NI_t - D_t$).

[9]The two consistency requirements are: First, the three elements of RI need to be consistently defined: Having specified the capital base (**$Capital_t$**), **$Earnings_t$** must be the income to that capital base in year t, and **r** must be the cost-of-capital associated with this source of capital. Second, the evolution of the capital base in this model must follow the Clean Surplus Relation (CSR).

[10]For example, Ohlson and Juettner-Nauroth [2005] and Easton [2004] use capitalized one-year-ahead earnings ($EARN_{t+1}$) as the starting capital base in developing the Abnormal Earnings Growth Model (AEGM). Bhojraj and Lee [2002] use the RIM formula to estimate a matching $PVRI$ for each firm's enterprise-value-to-sales (EV/S) ratio.

capital choice, we can derive an equivalent expression for the present value of the corresponding residual income term. In other words, for each *Capital$_t$* selected, we can compute a matching *PVRI$_t$* such that the sum will always be mathematically equivalent to the present value of future payout to shareholders.[11]

How might RIM help us to do fundamental analysis? For one thing, it gives us a much clearer view into the performance indicators that should drive market multiples. For example, dividing both sides of Equation (1) by a company's book value, we can re-express the price-to-book ratio in terms of expected ROEs:

$$\frac{P_t^*}{B_t} = 1 + \sum_{i=1}^{\infty} \frac{E_t[(ROE_{t+i} - r_e)B_{t+i-1}]}{(1 + r_e)^i B_t} \qquad (4.3)$$

where P_t^* is the present value of expected dividends at time t; $B_t =$ book value at time t; $E_t[.] =$ expectation based on information available at time t; $r_e =$ cost of equity capital; and $ROE_{t+i} =$ the after-tax return on book equity for period $t + i$.

This equation shows that a firm's price-to-book ratio is a function of its expected return on equity (ROE), its cost-of-capital (r_e) and its future growth rate in book value (which itself depends on future ROEs, and k, the dividend payout ratio).[12] Firms that have similar price-to-book ratios should have present values of future residual income (the infinite sum on the right-hand side of Equation (3)) that are close to each other.

Using the RIM framework outlined in Equation (3), Penman et al. [2014] demonstrate how accounting numbers are central for pricing

---

[11]Although the arithmetic carries through, clearly not all measures of capital are equally sensible from an economic perspective. A full analysis of which "capital-in-place" measures might be more sensible is beyond the scope of the current discussion. However, it might be worth noting in passing that granting greater latitude to management in reappraising balance sheet items could have the unhappy side effect of producing less comparable accounting rates-of-return, both for cross-sectional and for time-series analyses.

[12]Technically, it is not expected ROE per se, which appears in the formula, so much as the expected Net Income divided by the expected Book Value. Recall from the CSR, $B_{t+1} = B_t + NI_t - DIV_t = B_{t*}(1 + (1 - k)ROE_{t+1})$, therefore, the growth in book value is simply: $B_{t+1}/B_t = 1 + (1 - k)ROE_{t+1}$; where k is the payout ratio, DIV_t/NI_t.

because they influence expectations of forward earnings and subsequent earnings growth. Starting with a RIM representation, Penman et al. [2014] first show that the cost of equity capital collapses to a firm's forward earnings yield in the absence of earnings growth.

Of course, firms would be far easier to value in the absence of growth. However, the need for more granular valuation models stem from the fact that earnings growth varies in the cross-section. In the presence of growth, the Penman et al. [2014] framework helps illustrate that accounting knowledge is essential for pricing because it conveys information about expected earnings growth as well as the risks underlying these expectations. Below, we outline how investors can leverage the RIM framework to identify value by using accounting information to learn about the quality of a firm's earnings potential relative (that is, its quality) as well as the cost of the firm relative to its assets in place (that is, its cheapness).

4.4 The two sides of value investing

A key insight that falls directly from this analysis is that *value companies are not just those that are cheap relative to capital-in-place, but include those that are cheap relative to the present value of their future residual income.* A common misperception about value investing, at least among academics, is that it simply involves buying stocks that are cheap relative to measures of capital-in-place. For example, many academic studies (mostly from finance) define value stocks as firms that trade at lower market multiples of book value, earnings, or enterprise value (for example, $P/B, P/E, or EV/S$). Accounting-based valuation demonstrates the seriousness of this error, because cheapness (as expressed through lower market multiples) is only one (and arguably the much less interesting) part of value investing.

As the residual-income framework makes transparent, a firm's true fundamental value is made up of two key elements: Firm Value = Capital-in-place + Growth-opportunities. The problem with typical cheapness indicators is that they only compare the price of a stock to its capital-in-place (book value, capitalized-earnings, or sales), and miss entirely the second element in equity valuation.

The most successful fundamental investors, beginning with Ben Graham, have always viewed Value Investing as consisting of two key elements: (1) Finding "quality" companies, and (2) Buying them at "reasonable prices". In simple notation:

$$\textbf{\textit{Value Investing}} = \textbf{\textit{Cheapness}} + \textbf{\textit{Quality}}$$

A firm's market multiple is a measure of cheapness relative to assets-in-place, but that is the easier and arguably less interesting part of value investing. The more interesting part requires an investor to assess a firm's quality — that is, the present value of its expected future residual income (PVRI) relative to price, using various currently available performance indicators. That is, of course the heart of what we call fundamental analysis. The best fundamental investors focus on buying quality, for a given level of cheapness. It is in this spirit that Ben Graham built his original stock screen. Looking back at his quality factors (factors #6 to #10), Graham intuitively recognized that firms with lower leverage, higher liquidity, and a high rate of steady growth are those with the best chance of generating high rates of return in the future. Or, in RIM parlance, he believed that these are the high PVRI stocks.

4.5   Lessons from the field

This overarching theme of "cheapness + quality" is extremely helpful to bear in mind when trying to understand the investment approaches of investors, such as Warren Buffett, Charlie Munger, Joel Greenblatt, Julian Robertson, and a host of others who grew up under their tutelage (for example, the extremely successful "Tiger Cub" funds, such as Lone Pine, Viking, and Maverick Capital, all of which had their roots in Julian Robertson's Tiger Fund (1980–2000)). Let us consider one such example.

Joel Greenblatt and the Magic Formula

Joel Greenblatt is an American academic, hedge fund manager, investor, and writer. Like Graham, Greenblatt's career straddled academia and Wall Street. In 1985, he founded a hedge fund, Gotham

Capital, which focused on special situation investing. Greenblatt and his cofounder, Robert Goldstein, compounded Gotham's capital at a phenomenal 40% annually before fees for the 10 years from its formation in 1985 to its return of outside capital in 1995. After returning all outside capital, Greenblatt and Goldstein continued to invest their own capital in special situations. In 1999, he wrote his first best-seller, *You Can Be a Stock Market Genius*, which described the special situation investment strategy responsible for Gotham's success.

What Greenblatt is best known for, however, is his second book, *The Little Book That Beats the Market*. Published in 2005, the first edition sold over 300,000 copies and was translated into 16 languages, thus propelling Greenblatt to celebrity-investor status. As Greenblatt described it, this book was the product of an experiment, in which he wanted to see whether Warren Buffett's investment strategy could be quantified. He knew that the subtle qualitative judgment of "the Sage from Omaha" was probably beyond the reach of machines. Still, he wondered whether some of Buffett's magic might be bottled.

Studying Buffett's public pronouncements, most of which came in the form of Chairman's letters from Berkshire Hathaway, Inc., Greenblatt discerned a recurrent theme. As Buffett often quipped: *"It is far better to buy a wonderful company at a fair price than a fair company at a wonderful price."*[13] Buffett was not just buying cheap companies, Greenblatt observed, he was looking for quality companies at reasonable prices. What would happen if we tried to create a mechanical stock screen that invested in high-quality businesses trading at reasonable prices?[14]

The results were so impressive that in *The Little Book That Beats the Market*, Greenblatt called this strategy *The Magic Formula*. The details of the formula are laid out in Appendix 4.A. As you will see from this appendix, it is a remarkably simple strategy. Greenblatt ranked

---

[13]From the Chairman's Letter, Berkshire Hathaway, Inc., Annual Report, 1989.

[14]At least one other accounting academic came to the same conclusion about Buffett's investment strategy. In his 2010 book, *Buffett beyond Value*, Professor Prem Jain studied over 30 years of Buffett pronouncements and also came to the same conclusion [Jain, 2010]. Buffett favored quality growth (or in RIM parlance, high PVRI firms) over cheapness.

companies based on just two factors: Return-on-capital (ROC) and earnings-yield (EY). The Magic Formula, in a nutshell, looks for companies with a history of consistently high past ROC (five years of at least 20% annually), and bought the ones currently trading at the lowest earnings-yield. That's it!

Several points are worth noting. First, the formula works (or more precisely, it *has* worked for a long time). This basic formula has been thoroughly tested using U.S. data, both by Greenblatt and by others. Firms ranked at the top of this screen have outperformed their peers by a wide margin over the past 50 years.[15] Second, it is really *very similar* to what Ben Graham was doing many years earlier! Five years of high and consistent growth... low P/E ratios... sounds familiar? The more things change, the more they stay the same.

But of course, in the context of the RIM, all of this makes sense. Ben Graham, Warren Buffett, and Joel Greenblatt, they are all trying to do the same thing — find firms with high expected PVRI trading at reasonable market multiples. Consider Buffett's most often repeated four fold dictum: (1) Only invest in a business you can understand; (2) Look for companies with a sustainable competitive advantage, (3) Bet on companies with high-quality management teams, and (4) Buy with a good "Margin of Safety." The last point is easiest to understand and implement — buy firms with an attractive valuation relative to its capital base. What do the first three principles tell us? Are they not simply pointing us toward firms with a greater likelihood of high sustainable ROE's in the future? The verdict from the field is clear: Quality pays.

4.6 Empirical evidence from academic studies

Once we have the overarching valuation framework firmly in place, it is remarkable how well the evidence from empirical studies line up with the theory, and with the field evidence from investors. Let us now turn to this evidence.

---

[15] See for example, Gray and Carlisle [2013, Section 2] for a detailed replication of the formula using U.S. data from 1964 to 2011.

Cheapness

An enormous body of literature in accounting and finance documents the tendency of value stocks (stocks with low prices relative to their fundamentals) to outperform glamour stocks (stocks with high prices relative to their fundamentals). Common measures of value are the book-to-market ratio [Stattman, 1980, Rosenberg et al., 1985, Fama and French, 1992], the earnings-to-price ratio [Basu, 1977, Reinganum, 1981], the cashflow-to-price ratio [Lakonishok et al., 1994, Desai et al., 2004], and the sales-to-enterprise-value ratio [O'Shaughnessy, 2011]. The strength of the value effect varies over time and across stocks, but the broad tendency of value stocks to outperform glamour stocks is a highly robust finding in the academic literature.

While academics generally agree on the empirical facts, there is much less consensus on the reason behind these findings. Some feel the evidence clearly indicates that value stocks are underpriced (that is, they are bargains); others believe value stocks are cheap for a reason, and that common measures of value are also indicators of some sort of risk. For example, Fama and French [1992] suggest low price-to-book (P/B) stocks are more vulnerable to distress risk, and Zhang [2005] argues that these stocks have more "trapped assets," and are thus more susceptible to economic downturns.[16] Similarly, a related literature offers evidence that value and growth stocks possess differential sensitivities to time-varying macro-economic risks (see, for example, Vassalou [2003], Santos and Veronesi [2010], Campbell et al. [2010], Lettau and Wachter [2007], Da and Warachka [2009], Petkova and Zhang [2005]). We return to the role of risk and institutional frictions as an explanation for the value/glamour effect in more detail below.

Quality

The academic evidence in favor of quality investing has been perhaps a bit more difficult to recognize. Up to now, academics have not always agreed on what a quality firm might look like. Many papers have examined the persistence of earnings, for example, or the ability of accounting-based variables to predict future returns, but most have not done so under the quality rubric. Yet once we begin to piece

---

[16]For a much more detailed review of this debate, see Zacks [2011, Chapter 10].

together the evidence, and the composite sketch begins to fill it, the picture that emerges bears a remarkable resemblance to the indicators of quality as first expressed by Ben Graham in his original screen. Delightfully, the evidence also concords extremely well with what we might expect from valuation theory.

Holding a company's market multiple (for example, its price-to-book ratio) constant, what kind of firm *should* an investor pay more for? If we define quality firms as those that *deserve* a higher multiple, then valuation theory tells us the answer. According to the RIM, quality firms are those with a high present value of future residual income (high PVRI). The task of the empiricist is to examine which company characteristics, or perhaps performance metrics, might serve as useful indicators of future PVRI.

What are the key components of a company's PVRI? Of first order importance would be measures of future profitability and growth, since these elements are the primary drivers of firms' future ROE. Also important would be measures of safety. To the extent that safer firms deserve a lower cost-of-capital (r_e), and holding future expected cash flows constant, safer firms will deserve a higher PVRI. Finally, the expected rate of payout should play a role. Firms that maintain the same profitability and growth rates while paying back more capital to investors are, all else equal, deserving of a higher PVRI.

Note that we have thus far only discussed fundamental valuation, not market mispricing per se. Superior value estimation does not always translate into better returns prediction. This is because the latter involves a systematic mistake (some sort of error) in the current price; the former does not. It is possible that a historical indicator of quality (such as a firm's past ROE) is a strong predictor of future PVRI, but the market is aware of this and has appropriately priced it. In this case, we would not expect higher returns to an ROE-based strategy. Empirically, there are certainly seemingly sensible value + quality combinations that do not result in superior returns predictions. However, if prices generally converge toward fundamentals in the long run, we should expect better valuation estimates on average lead to superior returns prediction (see Lee et al., 1999 for a more detailed discussion).

Prior evidence is broadly consistent with these observations. In general, stable, safe, profitable firms with solid growth, good cash flows, lower risk, and higher payouts do in fact earn higher future returns. Below, we provide a brief survey of this evidence from prior research and discuss their relation to our overarching valuation framework.

Profitability and Growth

Piotroski [2000] shows that firms with better ROAs, operating cash flows, profit margins, and asset turnovers, consistently earn higher returns. Using eight fundamental indicators of firm performance and general health, he created a composite "F-Score." His evidence shows that F-Score is able to separate winners from losers from among stocks in the lowest P/B quintile (value stocks). Mohanram [2005] performs a similar exercise among high P/B firms (growth stocks) and find growing firms outperform firms with poor growth. Piotroski and So [2012] use the F-Score to show that the value/glamour effect is attributable to errors in market expectation about future fundamentals. Using $I/B/E/S$ analysts' forecasts, Frankel and Lee [1998] show that, holding P/B constant, firms with higher forecasted earnings earn higher returns, particularly when correcting for predictable errors in the analysts' consensus estimates. Overall, the evidence suggests that firms with higher profitability (past or forecasted) earn higher subsequent returns.

Earnings Quality

It is not simply the *quantity* of earnings that matters, the *quality* (the expected sustainability or persistence) of that earnings also matters. For example, Sloan [1996] and Richardson et al. [2005] show that the cash flow component of earnings is more persistent than the accrual component. Similarly, Hirshleifer et al. [2004] show that firms with a history of low cash profits relative to accounting profits significant underperform and this effect is incremental to results based on accruals as measured in Sloan [1996]. Novy-Marx [2013] shows that Gross Margin (Sales − Cost of Goods Sold) is an even better measure of core profits than bottom-line earnings. In this study, profitable firms generate significantly higher returns than unprofitable firms, despite having significantly higher valuation ratios.

Another line of research explores the usefulness of accounting numbers in identifying financial shenanigans. Beneish [1999] estimates an earning manipulation detection model based entirely on reported numbers from the period of alleged manipulation. In out-of-sample tests, Beneish et al. [BLN, 2013] show that this model correctly identified, in advance of public disclosure, a large majority (71%) of the most famous accounting fraud cases that surfaced after the model's estimation period. Perhaps even more significantly, BLN shows that the "probability of manipulation" (M-score) from the original Beneish model is a powerful predictor of out-of-sample stock returns — that is, firms that share traits with past earnings manipulators earn lower subsequent returns after controlling for multiple other factors, including accounting accruals.

Overall, these studies show that various accounting-based measures of cash flow profitability or earnings quality are even better predictors of future returns than simple measures based on reported earnings.

Safety

Safer stocks earn higher returns. This result is remarkably robust across many measures of safety. For example, *lower volatility* firms actually earn higher, not lower, returns [Falkenstein, 2012, Ang et al., 2006]. *Lower Beta* firms in fact earn higher returns [Black et al., 1972, Frazzini and Pedersen, 2014]. Firms with *lower leverage* earn higher returns [George and Hwang, 2010, Penman et al., 2007]. Most strikingly, firms with *lower levels of financial distress* also earn higher returns [Altman, 1968, Ohlson, 1980, Dichev, 1998, Campbell et al., 2008].[17] In short, firms that are safer, by many measures of safety, actually earn higher returns.

---

[17]Both Dichev [1998] and Campbell et al. [2008] find strong evidence that distress risk is actually *negatively* associated with subsequent returns. Dichev used Altman's Z-score and Ohlson's O-Score and show that going long in the 70% of firms with low bankruptcy risk, and shorting the remaining 30%, yields *positive* returns in 12 out of 15 years (1981–1995). Campbell et al. [2008] sort stocks into value-weighted portfolios by failure probability, and find that average excess returns are strongly, and almost monotonically, negatively related with the probability of failure. The safest 5% of stocks have an average excess yearly return of 3.4%, while the riskiest 1% of stocks have an average return of −17.0%.

Put simply, firms with higher volatility, higher Beta, higher leverage, and higher bankruptcy risk actually earn lower returns. This finding does not make sense in an equilibrium asset-pricing context — in equilibrium, firms with higher risk should be rewarded with higher future returns. However, the result makes perfect sense if we believe that these risk measures are associated with the discount rate markets used to compute a firm's PVRI. Viewed in this context, safer firms have lower cost-of-capital (r_e), and we would expect their PVRI (and thus their firm value) to be higher than the riskier firms, all else equal. If the market underappreciates a firm's true PVRI (as we have seen in the case of firms' Profitability and Growth indicators), then safer firms will in fact earn higher future realized returns.[18]

Payout

Finally, companies who make higher payouts to shareholders and creditors also earn higher future returns. For example, companies that repurchase their shares tend to do well [Baker and Wurgler, 2002, Pontiff and Woodgate, 2008, McLean et al., 2009], while firms that issue more shares tend to do worse [Loughran and Ritter, 1995, Spiess and Affleck-Graves, 1995]. A similar pattern is observed for debt issuances. Firms that issue more debt earn negative abnormal returns [Spiess and Affleck-Graves, 1999, Billett et al., 2006, Daniel and Titman, 2006], while firms that retire their debt earn positive abnormal returns [Affleck-Graves and Miller, 2003]. In fact, Bradshaw et al. [2006] show that it is possible to measure these effects using a measure of net external financing activities computed from companies' Statement of Cash Flow. Taken together, these findings are quite consistent with the RIM framework: firms that are returning capital at a faster rate (that is, firms with a higher dividend payout ratio) have more positive PVRI.

---

[18]Consistent with this argument, Chava and Purnanadam [2009] show that although distress risk is *negatively* correlated with future realized returns, it is *positively* correlated with a firm's market-implied cost of capital. In other words, the market *does* use a higher implied discount rate when discounting the future earnings of high distress firms; however, because these firms are still over-priced on average, they still earn lower future realized returns.

In short, what types of firms might be deemed higher quality? In other words, which firm characteristics are associated with higher future ROEs, lower cost-of-capital, and higher payouts? Prior studies suggest these are safe, profitable, growing firms that are also returning more of their capital to their investors. These facts are exactly what we would expect if markets underappreciate fundamental value, as reflected in current financial statements. They are much more difficult to reconcile with popular explanations of the value effect as a risk premium, as the quality firms are more profitable, less volatile, less prone to distress, have more persistent future cash flows, and lower levels of operating leverage. In a fascinating new study, Asness et al. [2013] pull these disparate strands of quality investing together. In this study, the authors define quality firms as stocks that are "safe, profitable, growing, and well-managed." They argue that all else equal investors should be willing to pay more for such firms. They show that in fact the market does not pay a high enough premium for these quality stocks. Sorting firms on the basis of their quality metric, they create a "Quality Minus Junk" (QMJ) portfolio, and find that this portfolio earns positive risk-adjusted returns in 22 out of 23 countries.

For their empirical tests, they compute a composite quality score for each firm based on the following 21 performance indicators, grouped into four categories. Each variable is ranked, and then normalized by subtracting its own mean and dividing by its own standard deviation:

I. Profitability (six variables) Bet in favor of firms with high *earnings* (ROA, ROE), high *gross-profit* (GPOA, GMAR), and high *operating cash flow* (CFOA, ACC). The numerators are current year earnings, gross margin, or operating cash flows; the denominators are total assets, book equity, total sales, or (in the case of ACC) total earnings.

II. Growth (six variables) Bet in favor of firms with the most *positive changes* in these profitability variables *over past five years* (for example, ΔGPOA $= (GP_t - GP_{t-5})/TA_{t-5}$), where GP = REV − COGS. In other words, Asness et al. [2013] define growth firms as those whose gross margin, or earnings, or cash flows, have grown the most over the past five years, relative to the year $t-5$ capital base.

III. Safety (six variables) Bet against firms with Beta (BETA), high volatility in returns and earnings (IVOL, EVOL), high leverage (LEV), and high levels of financial distress (*O*-Score, *Z*-Score). For this composite, the authors consolidate six measures of "safety" based on prior studies. In essence, safe firms are defined as those with low Beta, low volatility, low leverage, and low financial distress.

IV. Payout (3) Bet against firms with: high net equity issuance (EISS), high net debt issuance (DISS), low net payout ratio (NPOP) over past five years. Again, consistent with prior studies, Asness et al. [2013] define high payout firms in terms of net new issuances, plus dividends.

Notice how well these concepts map into the RIM framework. The first six indicators (past ROE, ROA, GPOA, GMAR, CFOA, and ACC) capture profitable firms that have higher gross margin, and a higher proportion of cash flow to accruals in their reported earnings. The next six indicators measure improvements in these variable dimensions of profitability. In the RIM framework, these 12 variables are all likely to be associated with higher future ROEs. Not surprisingly, Asness et al. [2013] find that these measures are strongly correlated with P/B ratios in the cross-section.

More interestingly, Asness et al. [2013] show that these variables also predict cross-sectional returns — that is, more profitable firms and firms with strong growth over the past five years consistently earn higher returns than firms with low profitability and low growth. To be fair, most of these variables have been reported by prior studies as being useful in returns prediction. Nevertheless, this study provides compelling evidence in support of the prediction from a simple RIM analysis — firms with high and persistent profits have high PVRI, and the market does not seem to fully price in this quality metric.

The main empirical finding in Asness et al. [2013] is that safer firms also earn higher future returns. They define safe firms as those with lower Beta, lower volatility (measured in terms of both idiosyncratic returns (IVOL) and past earnings (EVOL)), lower leverage (LEV), and lower financial distress (O-Score and Z-Score). While this result might be counter-intuitive for efficient market advocates, it is in fact quite easy to understand in terms of the RIM framework. Holding expected cash flows constant, safer firms are worth more (that is, they should have lower discount rates). To the extent that markets underappreciate this dimension of firm valuation, the safer firms would yield higher future returns.

Finally, Asness et al. [2013] show that firms with high net payouts (that is, those with low net equity issuances, low debt issuances, and high dividends) are also worth more. In the RIM framework, this is not surprising either. Firms which are able to produce the same level of growth as other firms while paying back more of their capital to investors are worth more. Again, when we measure the quality component of firm value (PVRI) more accurately, we are better able to identify firms that earn higher future returns.

4.7   Why does value investing continue to work?

Two stylized facts emerge from the preceding literature survey: (a) smart value investing, which incorporates both cheapness and quality, is associated with higher future stock returns, and (b) these strategies are being actively exploited by professional investors. These two findings naturally raise the issue of whether the value effect will persist in the future. Why haven't these effects been fully arbitraged away? Why does anyone continue to buy expensive, low-quality, stocks (that is, who buys "junk")?

Although a full treatment of this topic is probably beyond the scope of this section, the academic literature has proposed at least four reasons for the persistence of the value effect: (a) Risk-based Explanations, (b) Preference-based Explanations, (c) Institutional- and Friction-based Explanations, and (d) Behavioral-based Explanations. We briefly review these explanations below.

4.7.1   Risk-based explanations

The first, and longest-standing, explanation is that value stocks are simply riskier, and their higher future returns are a compensation for bearing this risk (see, for example, Fama and French [1992]). In support of this risk-based explanation, several studies provide evidence that value and growth stocks possess differential sensitivities to time-varying macroeconomic risks. For example, Vassalou [2003], Cohen et al. [2009], and Santos and Veronesi [2010] show that value stocks have greater sensitivities to economy-wide profitability than growth stocks. Similarly, Campbell et al. [2010] and Lettau and Wachter [2007] argue that growth (value) stocks display a higher sensitivity to discount rate (cash flow) news. Da and Warachka [2009] demonstrate that the sensitivities of firms' cash flows to aggregate earnings forecasts explain a significant portion of the value premium and Petkova and Zhang [2005] find that the value premium tends to covary positively with time-varying risk attributes. Lastly, Zhang [2005] argues that the value premium is driven by the differential ability of value and glamour firms to expand and contract their asset base in the face of changing economic conditions. Taken together, these papers suggest that some, if not all, of the documented return performance is an artifact of risk factor exposures that vary across value and glamour firms.

Surely we can agree that value investing involves some risk — that is, it is not a simple money pump. This is particularly true for the naïve form of value investing commonly discussed in the academic literature. The standard academic approach to value investing is to focus on a stock's cheapness (as measured by its market multiples). But cheap stocks (high B/M, high E/P, stocks for example) are typically priced that way for a reason — that is, the population of cheap stocks contain a disproportionately large number of low-quality firms. In fact, as Piotroski [2000, Table 1] showed, the median firm in the highest B/M quintile underperforms the market by over 6% over the next year — even though the mean return to these stocks is higher than the market. Naïve value does involve some risk, and this is borne out in the data.

The problem with the risk-based explanation is that, properly measured, value stocks are actually safer than the growth stocks. Once we incorporate measures of quality, it is clear that value investing does not generally incur higher risk, on average, at least by most sensible measure of risk (see, for example, Piotroski and So [2012]). The studies surveyed earlier strongly suggest that in fact stocks with more stable cash flows, lower financial distress, lower Beta, and lower volatility actually earn higher future realized returns. Certainly, there is no doubt that risk may be part of the explanation for these findings, however, our point is that a preponderance of evidence linking returns to indicators of value is difficult to fully reconcile with risk-based explanations.

4.7.2   Preference-based explanations

According to this explanation, some investors *have a preference for* stocks with "lottery-like" payoffs — that is, return distributions that are right-skewed. Stocks that have these features will therefore, all else equal, appear "over-priced" in a mean–variance world [Brunnermeier and Parker, 2005, Brunnermeier et al., 2007]. Bali et al. [2011] provide evidence consistent with this phenomenon, and Kumar [2009] shows this effect applies particularly to retail traders.

It seems plausible that a subset of investors might have preferences beyond the mean–variance tradeoff considered by standard asset-pricing models. For example, investors may behave as if they prefer lottery-like payoffs, however, it might be difficult to empirically separate this explanation from some of the behavioral-based explanations below (in fact, the literature on Information Uncertainty [Jiang et al., 2005, Zhang, 2005] makes the same point in a behavioral context). But if investors do exhibit an innate preference for lottery-like stocks, the value effect will, of course, be likely to persist well into the future.

4.7.3   Institutional- and friction-based explanations

A. Liquidity-driven Price Pressures

Stock prices are constantly buffeted by non-fundamental price pressures. Sometimes capital flows into or out of an asset simply "herd" in the same direction for liquidity reasons. These provide both opportunities and challenges for value investors.

For example, in Coval and Stafford [2007]: "Fire sales" by mutual funds that face redemption pressure due to weak performance in prior quarters can depress the prices of the stocks they own — and these stocks subsequently rebound strongly. Non-fundamental flows should reverse over time, and may not be driven by cognitive biases. The impact of these non-fundamental price changes is not specific to value investing, however, it will contribute to a higher return:risk ratio for investors who trade on value indicators.

B. Prudent-Man Concerns

Del Guercio [1996] notes that institutional investors may gravitate toward glamour stocks due to "prudent-man" concerns, which refers to the idea that investments in high profile, glamour stocks are easier to justify as sound decisions (that is, they make the investor appear prudent). Skewness in institutional investors' portfolios toward high profile firms can exacerbate the value effect by raising demand for glamour stocks. Similarly, as noted in Green et al. [2011] and So [2013], to the extent that mispricing emerges because investors equate good companies with good investments, glamour stocks may offer greater ex-post justifiability in case of losses.[19]

Thus, prudent-man concerns can contribute to the persistence of the value effect because institutional investors concerned with their reputations, legal liabilities, and/or client relationships with sponsors may fail to buy value stocks and sell glamour stocks because potential losses may be harder to justify as prudent investments.

C. Limits to Arbitrage

Broadly speaking, the value effect may continue to exist because there are limits to arbitrage. In finance textbooks, arbitrage is described as a riskless investment position from simultaneously buying and selling securities, typically requiring no capital investment. This form of textbook arbitrage is commonly referred to as 'deterministic' arbitrage.

---

[19]This positive link between a firm's profile and glamour status is also consistent with the model of capital equilibrium under incomplete information in Merton [1987], which shows that firm value is an increasing function of investor recognition of the firm. See Lehavy and Sloan [2008] for related evidence on the empirical link between investor recognition and expected returns.

In practice, investors capitalize on the value effect through 'statistical' arbitrage, which refers to trades based on statistical evidence of mispricing with respect to the expected value of a given asset. Statistical arbitrage, by contrast, entails significant risks. As noted earlier, although value investing tends to yield positive returns, Piotroski [2000] shows that the median return to holding value firms is negative.

A related form of risk involved with statistical arbitrage is that the returns to value-based strategies are earned over longer holding periods, which reflects the fact that underpriced value firms tend to only gradually rise toward their expected value and overpriced glamour firms tend to only gradually fall toward their expected value. Thus, profiting from the value effect can require significant patience and capital deployment. Shleifer and Vishny [1997] point out that the arbitrage mechanism is constrained because investors withdraw money from investment funds that lose money, even if the losses result from a predictably temporary increase in mispricing. Stocks often reach value (glamour) status in response to upward (downward) revisions in prices, thus, a related risk in value investing is that profiting from underpriced securities may require betting against negative momentum and vice versa for glamour stocks.

Related evidence in Brunnermeier and Nagel [2004] shows that several prominent hedge funds bet against the Internet bubble in spring 1999 and suffered significant losses and capital outflows as the bubble continued and mispricing deepened. This example illustrates one of the central difficulties in arbitraging the value effect: the uncertainty over when mispricing will correct. When investors' investment horizon is short, the value effect may persist because the market lacks the sufficient patience to commit the capital necessary to discipline prices. We discuss related evidence on the limits of arbitrage in more detail in Section 5 of the second volume of this book.

4.7.4 Behavioral-based explanations

The final, and in our view most intriguing, set of explanations for the value effect is rooted in human cognitive behavior. While not mutually exclusive, we group these explanations into four sub-categories.

A. Saliency vs. Weight

Human decision making under uncertainty involves assessing the probability of alternative outcomes. A recurrent theme in cognitive psychology is that human subjects consistently under-weight the probability of certain types of events and over-weight the probability of others. In their seminal study, Griffin and Tversky [1992] show that signals with high statistical reliability (high "weight") but are not salient (low "saliency") are consistently underweighted. Conversely, highly salient signals with low statistical reliability are often overweighted. Apparently, Bayesian updating is a difficult cognitive task.

Apply this concept to value investing, firm attributes that are "boring" (non-salient) receive less-than-optimal weight, and those that are "glamorous" (salient) receive more-than-optimal weight. The historical indicators of quality discussed earlier are weighty in terms of their statistical association with future residual income (that is, sustainable cash flows), but they may not receive sufficient weight in the minds of the investors. Value-based arbitrageurs help to reduce the mispricing, but new "story stocks" arise on a daily basis as markets seek to assimilate the constant flow of news items and/or pseudosignals.

B. Extrapolation

A related behavioral explanation points to evidence in the psychology literature documenting the tendency of individuals to over-extrapolate past trends (see, for example, Griffin and Tversky [1992]). This literature asserts that investors underestimate the tendency for trends in firms' past performance to mean revert and overestimate the tendency for them to continue. Lakonishok et al. [1994] apply this insight to the pricing of stocks and provide evidence that the value effect is a result of judgment errors where investors overestimate the persistence of past trends in firm performance when valuing firms' future cash flows. Related evidence in Dechow and Sloan [1997] shows that analysts tend to fixate on past earnings growth when forecasting future earnings and that investors tend to naively rely on analysts' forecasts.

By overestimating the tendency of trends to continue, investors extrapolate past growth too far leading to upwardly biased prices for glamour stocks and similarly over-extrapolate past underperformance leading to downward-biased prices for value stocks. Under this explanation, investors place excessive weight on recent history and underweight the likelihood of mean reversion in firms' performance.

C. Momentum (Positive Feedback) Trading

All pure value investors face the risk that noise trading will push prices even further from fundamental value. Value stocks tend to be negative momentum stocks — and over at least mid-horizon (three to 12 months) holding periods, value bets run into a momentum headwind.

Strongly negative sentiment typically accompanies really attractive buys based on fundamentals (for recent examples, consider the risk associated with buying Greek assets, or debt instruments issued by U.S. financial service firms, during the global crisis). Thus value inherently faces greater short- and mid-horizon risk from positive feedback trading. The extent to which this matters depends on the holding horizon and the stability and depth of his/her source of capital.

D. Over-confidence in High "Information Uncertainty" Settings

Finally, the evidence is clear that firms operating in high "information uncertainty" (IU) settings tend to earn lower subsequent returns. For example, Jiang et al. [2005] define IU in terms of "value ambiguity," or the precision with which firm value can be estimated by knowledgeable investors at reasonable cost. In Jiang et al. [2005], as well as Zhang [2005], high-IU firms earn lower future returns. In addition, high-IU firms exhibit stronger price as well as earnings momentum effects. Specifically, younger firms, firms with higher volatility, higher volume (that is, turnover), greater expected growth, higher price-to-book, wider dispersion in analyst earnings forecasts, and longer implied duration in future cash flows all earn lower returns. In some sense, each of the above phenomena is related to firms' IU measure.

Jiang et al. [2005] argue that all these observations can be traced back to the same behavioral root: People are more overconfident in settings with high "information uncertainty". Applied to value investing, investors tend to overweight elements of firm value that are further out into the future, and underweight those that are nearer at hand (in other words, they use too low implied discount rate when valuing firm future cash flows). This leads to a tendency to overprice "story stocks" whose cash flows are expected further out into the future.

The overconfidence hypothesis would help to explain why strategies based on the ratio of short-duration expected cash flows relative to stock prices can generate higher returns. For example, the evidence in Frankel and Lee [1998] that holding P/B constant, firms with higher forecasted near-term earnings earn higher returns, which is consistent with investors underweighting value-relevant information that is nearer at hand. It would also suggest an explanation for why momentum effects are stronger in high-IU settings.

Summary

Since the days of Benjamin Graham over 80 years ago, fundamental investors have served as a stabilizing force in financial markets. In this article, we reviewed the theoretical foundations of this style of investing including an accounting-based valuation framework for reconciling the vast empirical evidence. We have also attempted to reconcile the investment approaches of some well-known fundamental investors with recent findings from academia.

A number of recent studies provide compelling evidence that historical accounting numbers are informative, and are already playing a useful role in fundamental investing. For example, none of the 21 indicators in the composite quality index featured in Asness et al. [2013] rely on a company's stock price. They are all variables constructed from historical GAAP-based financial statements. Yet together these variables provide a good composite sketch of companies that tend to earn higher returns in the future.

The RIM helps us to understand why. Careful fundamental analysis can help us to derive performance measures that help predict the future profitability and growth of firms. It can also help us assess the riskiness of a firm, as well as its likely future payout to shareholders. In short, accounting information can help us to evaluate not only the first moment of a firm's future cash flows (that is, the numerator of the future payoffs), but also its second moment (that is, the riskiness of these payoffs). As valuation theory shows, both elements are useful in evaluating the present value of a firm's future growth opportunities. In fact, the key predictions from valuation theory dovetail nicely, not only with recent empirical findings in academia, but also with the age-old wisdom espoused by many savvy investors.

We might not be there yet, but we are good ways down the road mapped out for us by Ben Graham almost 80 years ago. The verdict from the field agrees with the verdict from the ivory tower. Buy quality firms at reasonable prices, and use historical accounting numbers to help you achieve that task. It will give you an edge in your investing, and help make markets more efficient as well!

Appendix 4.A

Joel Greenblatt's Magic Formula

The following basic instructions for the Magic Formula are extracted from *The Little Book That Still Beats the Market*, written by Joel Greenblatt and published in 2010. They are included here for illustrative purposes. Interested readers are encouraged to either buy the book or visit Greenblatt's website: magicformulainvesting.com for more details.

Greenblatt's Basic Principle:

- Buy good businesses (high return on capital) at bargain prices (high earnings yield).

- Do this consistently by maintaining a portfolio of 20 to 30 stocks, and spreading out the timing of your purchases (buy a few stocks each month throughout the year).

- Hold the winners for at least one year (for tax efficiency reasons).

Implementing Greenblatt's "Magic Formula"

- Look for companies with an average ROC of 20% or higher over the past five years (see below for details on ROC calculation).

- Among these, pick those ones with the highest earnings-yield (EY).

- Limit stocks to those with at least $200m in Market Cap; Exclude Utilities; Financials; ADRs; and firms that have reported earnings within the past week.

- Also consider excluding firms with and earnings yield in excess of 20% (which may indicate a data problem or an unusual situation).

Detailed Factor Definitions:

- *Return-on-Capital (ROC) = EBIT/Capital*

    Where EBIT is Earnings before interest and taxes, and Capital is defined as: Net PP&E + Net Working Capital.

- *Earnings Yield (EY) = EBIT/TEV*

    Where EBIT is Earnings before interest and taxes, and TEV is defined as: Market capitalization + total debt — excess cash + preferred stock + minority interests (excess cash is cash + current assets − current liabilities).

5

Arbitrage Costs

This section discusses some of the more important costs and constraints faced by smart money seeking to conduct rational informational arbitrage. We have two objectives: (1) to explain to an academic audience some of the practical challenges faced by professional fund managers engaged in active investing; and (2) to compile a source of academic references for both academics and financial professionals interested in better understanding the current state of the literature on limits-to-arbitrage.

Arbitrage costs are far less understood/appreciated in academia than in practice. Many academics find it difficult to understand why a flood of smart money does not immediately rush forth to extinguish mispricings as soon as they appear. After all, as Cochrane [2011, p. 1070] observed, "one person's fire sale is another's buying opportunity." In a frictionless world, if a fire sale occurs, an army of bargain hunters would swoop in and the price dislocation would disappear almost as soon as it appeared. That is what academics believe *should* happen. Many also believe that it is a reasonable description of what *does* happen in reality.

The active asset manager's view of arbitrage costs is quite different. Active asset managers are in the business of identifying and exploiting price dislocations. However, their everyday efforts to profit from such opportunities face a myriad of challenges and constraints. These challenges and constraints limit the precision with which they can place their bets and the amount of capital they can access and deploy. They expend most of their efforts and resources on dealing with these constraints. In fact, most active asset managers we know are continuously investigating new ways to reduce arbitrage costs, manage risks, and improve their informational edge. To them, limits to arbitrage are a daily reality.

The difference between these two perspectives is due, in part, to differences in the level of granularity each group aspires to achieve. The exact type of cost and risk that matters most to an active investor will vary by investment strategy. An arbitrageur involved in high-frequency trading will have a different set of concerns from a long-term value investor, and someone engaged in convertible bond arbitrage will have still another set of concerns. Therefore a more detailed study of arbitrage costs needs to proceed strategy-by-strategy. Yet such detailed analyses are typically beyond the means/interest of non-practitioners. At the same time, this type of analysis can run counter to the academic prerogative to stay on key to broader conceptual themes. As a result, many academic discussions of arbitrage costs have remained at a relatively high level of abstraction.

In this section, we follow a simple organizing framework that tries to reach a balance between the needs of the two groups. First, to set the stage, we begin with a short description of professional money management as an information-based business. The goal of this brief narrative is to provide a context for a more detailed discussion of arbitrage costs.

Next, we discuss three types of costs that are common to all active investors. Specifically, we group arbitrage constraints into the costs and risks associated with: (1) *identifying/verifying the mispricing*, (2) *implementing/executing the strategy*, and (3) *financing/funding the business*. These three types of costs apply to any professional asset manager seeking to profit from market mispricing. While the relative importance of each cost category will vary from strategy to strategy, all active investors need to invest resources to identify the mispricing, as well as to implement/execute and finance/fund their strategies.

Our central message is that real-world arbitrage is an information game that involves a constantly improving technology. Asset managers face substantial uncertainty and risk whenever they try to identify/verify, finance/fund, and execute/implement an active strategy. At every stage of this process, they need better (more precise; more reliable) information. The right kind of information can help asset managers to identify mispricing, reduce risk, secure funding, and improve trade execution.

Among these three types of costs, perhaps least understood are the costs associated with strategy (or mispricing) identification. When academics discuss limits to arbitrage, the focus is usually on either execution/trading costs (see, for example, Keim and Madhavan [1997] and Beneish et al. [2015]), or financing/funding constraints (see, for example, Shleifer and Vishny [1997], Shleifer and Vishny [2011], Acharya and Pedersen [2005], and Hu et al. [2013]). While these costs are important, much of the professional asset manager's concern is on identifying and calibrating the pricing error itself. In particular, they are interested in the quality of the information used to formulate their bets, and the costs associated with obtaining that information.[1]

On the subject of strategy identification, mounting academic evidence suggests that financial markets have a limited ability to fully process more complex news events. Classic economic theory assumes that individuals are fully rational and unravel complex gambles/bets at little or no cost. Building on this foundation, traditional asset-pricing models typically conclude that market prices incorporate all publicly available information quickly at minimal cost. However, a growing body of evidence suggests that these assumptions may be seriously flawed.

---

[1]By "quality of information" in the mispricing context, we mean the precision and accuracy with which parameters/variables crucial to the investment strategy can be estimated. As we discuss later, this includes information related to the availability of asset that can serve as close substitutes.

Many recent studies are finding that incomplete processing of public news is much more likely to occur when the signal is either more difficult to unravel/decipher, or when the market is distracted by other competing stimulants. In these situations, newly-arrived information is more likely to be misprocessed, leading to predictable patterns in future returns. Specifically, recent studies related to: (a) investor limited attention, (b) task complexity, and (c) information uncertainty, show that all three factors can play a role in confounding the market's ability to fully process new information.

In the limited attention literature, for example, a number of studies show that earnings news is processed more fully when there are fewer competing stimulants [Francis et al., 1992, Bagnoli et al., 2005, Della Vigna and Pollet, 2009, Hirshleifer et al., 2009]. When such stimulants are present, the contemporaneous response to earnings news is more muted, and post-announcement price drift is more pronounced. Even distractions such as the NCAA basketball tournament can have a notable negative effect on the market's ability to fully process earnings news [Drake et al., 2015].

In addition, many studies show that the market appears to have trouble dealing with more subtle/nuanced/complex aspects of news events. The evidence spans a wide range of different news or information signals, including: Non-routine insider trades [Cohen et al., 2012]; highly-innovative analyst forecast revisions [Gleason and Lee, 2003]; more-reliable accrual measures [Richardson et al., 2005]; better-connected board members [Larcker et al., 2013]; slow-moving demographic data [Della Vigna and Pollet, 2007]; more-productive R&D expenses [Cohen et al., 2013a]; and even the relative saliency of past price momentum patterns [Da et al., 2015]. In each case, market participants seem to have a cursory understanding of the news, as evidenced by an initial price or trading volume reaction. However, it appears that the initial reaction is incomplete and the market misses some, often more subtle, dimension of the news signal. As a result, prices do not fully incorporate the news, leading to predictable returns, often of significant economic magnitude.

Similarly, the information uncertainty (IU) literature shows that higher uncertainty firms are consistently associated with greater degrees of mispricing.[2] Specifically, these companies experience lower mean future returns and stronger price momentum effects, consistent with greater investor overconfidence in high-IU firms [Jiang et al., 2005, Zhang, 2006a]. The analysts covering high-IU firms also appear to issue more overoptimistic earnings forecasts than those covering low-IU firms [Zhang, 2006b].

The main stylized fact that emerges from these studies is that informational complexity matters. Financial markets appear to have limited bandwidth or capacity to process many types of information in a timely manner. As a result, simpler/more-salient signals are more likely to be fully processed than complex/subtle ones. Although markets do appear to learn about some of these patterns over time, the corrective process is not instantaneous, and predictable patterns in future returns can persist for many years.[3]

5.1 What the smart money sees

As a professional fund manager engaged in informational arbitrage, what costs and risks do you face? Let us assume the role of someone who believes (s)he has identified an economically important type of mispricing.

Suppose you take the plunge and start a small hedge fund business. As a startup fund, you will have the usual overhead costs of a new business, including legal fees, office rental costs, and accounting/operational expenses. Each month you have to pay for operating costs such as data feeds, prime broker costs, processing costs, compliance costs, and financing charges. Unless you can run the entire operation alone you

---

[2]High-IU firms are younger, smaller, more volatile, greater trading volume (turnover), have more volatile past earnings, as well as greater dispersion in analyst forecasts of future earnings.

[3]Several studies document gradual erosion in the profitability of anomaly-based strategies. For example, Green et al. [2011] discuss the demise of the Sloan [1996] accrual anomaly as capital invested by hedge funds increasingly focused on extreme accrual firms over the years. Bebchuk et al. [2013] report a similar finding for a trading strategy based on corporate governance. More generally, McLean and Pontiff [2013] survey 82 strategies identified in academic research that predict returns. They report that post-publication predictability significantly declines, while trading activity associated with the strategies significantly increases.

will need to attract the right talent, and you need to raise sufficient capital to ensure that they are paid.

In attempting to raise capital, you will encounter well-documented agency problems [Shleifer and Vishny, 1997]. Specifically, your capital providers will typically not have the same understanding of your strategy as you do. You will need to convince them to trust you with their money. You will need to knock on doors and spend time meeting with prospective clients. If you run a quantitative strategy, you will find that "back-tested" evidence is typically met with skepticism ("I have never seen a bad back-test"). If your history as a fund manager (that is, your "track record") is short, you will have your work cut out for you to prove that you can consistently generate returns while mitigating the attendant risks.

Even if you manage to raise some seed capital, it could be quickly withdrawn if you do not get off to a good start. Because prices are noisy, and do not always converge quickly to value, you face short-term mortality risk due to bad luck or an even larger divergence between value and price. This can happen even if your strategy is rational and long-term viable [Brunnermeier and Nagel, 2004]. You may even have your capital withdrawn from you precisely when it is most likely to earn a higher return [Shleifer and Vishny, 1997].

Another problem you will discover is that the information you have about the strategy is noisy. Because of incomplete information (aka "limited attention"), you might not be aware of important but relevant facts that are known to others. You believe that a particular asset is being sold at fire sale prices. But you may learn later that the seller knows something you do not know, and what looked like a sure bet maybe no bargain at all [Mitchell et al., 2002]. Even when what you have identified is an actual bargain, there may be no good substitute asset with which to hedge the bet, and your less-than-perfect substitute could bring about your downfall before you can close your position (think Long-Term Capital). You may also underestimate your trading costs, or have difficulty borrowing the requisite shares you wish to short [Beneish et al., 2015].

If initial performance is only fair to middling, you will have serious problems retaining your talent and keeping everyone motivated. But if initial performance is good to excellent, you will face other challenges. You will have to handle increasingly complex demands from your growing set of clients (the bigger ones will now demand "separate accounts"[4]). You will have to fend off new competitors, particularly defectors from your own team, who can become your keenest competitors. As asset-under-management increases, you will also need to manage overall firm growth, hire/onboard new personnel, and deal with increasingly complicated regulations. Importantly, you will also need to gauge the right size and scale (that is, the "capacity") of the strategy, which directly impacts your performance [Berk and van Binsbergen, 2014]. Finally, you will need to do all this while having only a vague and imperfect sense of how "crowded" your investment space has become [Stein, 2009].

Each of these steps is costly and involves some risk. All active asset managers must manage these costs and risks while focusing sharply on the extraction of a particular form of mispricing. Many will fail, even if they had correctly identified a market pricing inefficiency of both statistical and economical significance.

This noisy and flawed process of informational arbitrage is the "DNA" of financial markets. The technologies and tactics employed by these asset managers are what give our financial markets their character. Even in our most liquid markets with asset managers that apply state-of-the-art technology, research shows that a good deal of mispricing can remain in equilibrium, because it is simply too costly to be eliminated fully.[5] It is in the daily management of these arbitrage costs

---

[4]In a simple setting, the asset manager maintains a single "commingled fund" on behalf of all clients. The pooling of client assets into a single portfolio greatly simplifies trading and book-keeping functions. However some clients, particularly large ones, may ask for a separate account. In a separate account arrangement, each client's fund is kept separated from the funds of others. The asset manager would then need to ensure that each account is updated on a timely basis, and that all clients are treated fairly as the "model portfolio" is rebalanced. Daily trade settlements and account reconciliations become increasingly complex as the number of separate accounts grows.

[5]In the most liquid markets, such as the auctions for U.S. Treasury securities [Lou et al., 2013] or the primary market for Exchange-Traded Funds [Madhavan and Sobczyk, 2014], these costs can still limit the deployment of arbitrage capital.

that individual active managers, and in turn our financial markets, produce a "somewhat-efficient" price for each asset.

5.2   Strategy identification and verification

The first task of a would-be arbitrageur is to identify and verify a potentially profitable strategy. When a discrepancy is observed between the market price of an asset and its estimated theoretical value, there are two possibilities. The first is that the market price is wrong and the discrepancy represents a trading opportunity. The second is that the theoretical value is wrong and the discrepancy is due to a mistake in the valuation method. How can an active investor tell the difference?

In the next sub-section, we discuss the importance of having substitute (or near-substitute) assets. We show that even if it is not possible for an arbitrageur to be absolutely sure about a mispricing, the existence of near-substitute assets can greatly reduce his/her risk. In fact, when there are no "natural substitutes," professional arbitrageurs will look for ways to create "synthetic near-substitutes." The trade will then consist of a long (or a short) in the asset that appears mispriced, and an offsetting position in the substitute asset. This basic approach underpins most of the active strategies carried out by hedge funds in equity and fixed income markets.

5.2.1   Availability of substitutes

Mispricings are much easier to identify/verify when the asset in question has close substitutes (or a set of "reference assets" whose prices track closely together). The closer is the substitutability between an asset and its reference asset(s), the more precisely mispricing can be identified and exploited. When an asset has no close substitutes, informational arbitrage is inherently risky and we can expect the "corridor of arbitrage" (the absolute magnitude of the mispricing) to be relatively wide. In other words, assets with no ready substitutes will be much more loosely tethered to their fundamental values.

Given this simple principle, it is not surprising to see that the price of an exchange-traded fund (ETF), for example, is closely tied to the net-asset-value of the underlying basket of composite securities. Similarly, we should not be surprised that the prices of highly-liquid equity option contracts generally track their theoretical prices based on option-pricing models; or that long-duration bonds with similar maturities from the same issuer trade at similar premiums or discounts. These are, after all, assets with close substitutes.

Things become more complicated when the assets are less-than-perfect substitutes. What, for example, is a close substitute for a share in Google? Or Linked-In? Or Tesla Motors? In the realm of equities, each share is a fractional ownership claim on an operating business with an indefinite life span. Such claims typically do not have perfect substitutes, and accordingly, we often observe share prices in stock markets that seem disconnected from sensible value estimates based on projected cash flows. Betting that such apparent price dislocations will correct within a reasonable time horizon is, of course, a risky proposition.

One way to reduce the risk in equity investing, and create more precise firm-specific bets, is by hedging out the common sources of co-movement among stocks and thus targeting the idiosyncratic component of returns. For example, a long position in Google can be viewed as a bet on a set of common factors that drive Google's stock returns, plus a bet on Google's residual return (that is, the idiosyncratic component of its return). Using risk factors that are common to academic studies, we can express Google's monthly returns as follows:

$$R_t^{GOOG} = \alpha + \beta^M R_t^M + \beta^{HML} R_t^{HML} + \beta^{SMB} R_t^{SMB} + \beta^{Tech} R_T^{Tech} + \varepsilon_t$$

Where R^{GOOG} is Google's excess return, R^M is the excess return of the market, R^{HML} is the return on a value strategy, R^{SMB} is the return on a size strategy, and R^{Tech} is the return on the information technology sector relative to the return on the market portfolio.

A monthly time-series regression of this form will yield a relatively high adjusted r-squared, somewhere in the neighborhood of 60%. In other words, much of the volatility from owning Google shares derives from their correlation with M (the market portfolio), HML (the value-to-growth tilt), SMB (the size tilt), and $Tech$ (the technology industry). Whether this co-movement is due to fundamentals or investor sentiment is less germane. The more important point is that, if these correlation patterns are at all stable, we will now be able to construct a substitute asset, essentially a "synthetic" Google, based on them.

The idea is quite simple. When we buy a share of Google, we will short (or long) the right amount of R, *HML*, *SMB*, and *Tech*, to exactly offset the incremental exposure of our portfolio to these common factors. Because Google is a large-cap technology stock with a relatively low book-to-market ratio, we will most likely need to short R and *Tech*, and long *HML* and *SMB*. Taken together, the two legs of this trade (long GOOG and short the synthetic) will result in a focused bet on Google-specific mispricing and a much smaller net increase in the volatility of our portfolio than if we had simply taken a long position in GOOG. Presto! We have just created a more focused stock-selection strategy by improving the substitutability of the assets in our investable universe.

What we have done in the case of a single stock can be generalized to a basket of stocks. With the help of a commercially available equity risk model (from, for example, MSCI Barra, or Axioma, or Northfield), asset managers can create equity portfolios that have a lot, or very little, exposure to each of the risk factors in the model. Working in their favor is the fact that equity returns feature a large common component. By adjusting the weights on the individual positions (that is, the number of shares of each firm held), an equity asset manager with firm-specific insights can hedge out much of the portfolio volatility due to industry or style-based factors. The final portfolio is much more efficient, in terms of its volatility-to-expected-return ratio, than one that only holds long positions.[6]

To summarize, by reducing the sources of incidental risk in their portfolio, asset managers can focus more sharply on identifying firm-specific mispricings. For example, an asset manager might have a dim view on the operating cash flow (OCF) of a fast-growing restaurant chain. She believes that the current OCF is at an unsustainable level, and that the company is likely to miss earnings, either for the current

---

[6]Readers interested in going deeper on the finer points of portfolio construction and risk management in an equity context are strongly encouraged to read the original classic by Grinold and Kahn [1999], or more recent adaptations, such as Qian et al. [2007] and Zhou and Jain [2014].

or for the next quarter. This manager can short the firm, and simultaneously long a basket of restaurant stocks that exactly offset the offending firm's exposure to multiple factors. The net result is a purer bet on the firm-specific insight that gave rise to the original trade. If the manager wishes, she can now lever up her bet to bring the total risk of the portfolio back to the level it would have been at had she simply shorted the stock.

5.2.2 Other active strategies

The same principle of trading "near-enough" substitutes carries to other settings. The following are a few examples either from an academic study or from the hedge fund industry, or both.

Statistical Arbitrage Statistical arbitrage strategies bet on price reversion between stocks that have similar attributes. For example, in a simple "pairs trading" strategy, traders look for pairs of stocks whose returns tend to be highly correlated [Goetzmann and Rouwenhorst, 2006]. When their prices diverge sufficiently relative to historical reference points, these traders bet on a convergence by buying the stock that appears cheap and shorting the stock that appears too expensive. In more sophisticated versions of such strategies, traders identify "peer" firms using an array of firm characteristics, or statistical co-integration techniques, and bet on the stocks whose recent returns deviate most from the returns of their "peer" firms.

Negative Stub Value Trades Mitchell et al. [2002] examine 82 "negative stub value" situations, where the market value of a company is less than its subsidiary. These situations would seem to be ideal arbitrage opportunities, whereby smart money investors can buy the parent and short the subsidiary. Unfortunately, although some of these cases yielded positive returns, the substitution between parent and sub is less than perfect. For 30% of the sample, the link between the parent and its subsidiary is severed before the relative value discrepancy is corrected. Furthermore, the path to convergence can be neither smooth nor swift. The authors conclude that arbitrage is limited by the uncertainty over the distribution of returns and characteristics of the accompanying risks.

Convertible Bond Arbitrage A convertible bond is a corporate bond that can be converted into stock. It is most simply viewed as a straight bond plus a call option to buy a newly issued share at a fixed price. Most convertible bond traders rely on this simple identity to look for a relative mispricing between a convertible bond and its underlying stock. Perhaps because of investor inattention, convertible bonds tend to be less liquid and trade at a discount relative to the underlying stock. Option-pricing techniques are used to identify the mispricings, and the trader buys the convertible bond and hedges it by shorting the stock.

Pedersen [2015, Chapter 15] contains an excellent discussion of this strategy. As he writes, "the cheapness of convertible bonds is at an efficiently inefficient level that reflects the supply and demand for liquidity... (w)hen the supply of convertible bonds is large relative hedge funds' capital and access to leverage, then the cheapness increases. For instance, when convertible bond hedge funds face large redemptions, or when their bankers pull financing, then convertible bonds become very cheap and illiquid." (p. 271).

In all these examples, and there are many others like them, the active investor uses a "near-enough substitute" to help *identify* a mispricing, or to *implement* a strategy, sometimes both. If the substitution is extremely close, the residual risk can become quite low, and the investor can apply leverage to return the strategy to a target risk level.

In cases where close substitutes are not available, traders would need to either be willing to take large unhedged bets (a prime example is Global Macro Investing, in which investors take directional bets on an entire market or an asset class), or limit their risk by trading in and out of any given security quickly (for example, managed future strategies that rely on time-series momentum techniques).[7]

---

[7]In directional macro strategies, the volatile nature of the payoff is a very real constraint in the deployment of capital (see Pedersen, 2015, Chapter 11 for details). In managed future strategies, investors typically make many relatively short duration bets across multiple asset classes, again with the goal of risk reduction in mind (see Pedersen, 2015, Chapter 12 for details).

5.3 The role of complexity

Academic studies have identified a number of factors that seem to increase the likelihood of erroneous inferences by investors, irrespective of the underlying strategy. Broadly speaking, this literature shows that search costs and task complexity has an impact on the likelihood and magnitude of mispricings. We discuss these factors under three sub-headings: (1) Limited attention; (2) Task complexity; and (3) Information uncertainty.

5.3.1 Limited attention

Many empirical findings suggest that investors do not take into account all relevant information when making decisions. For example, prices seem to underreact to earnings news [Bernard and Thomas, 1990], but also overreact to accruals, which is a component of earnings [Sloan, 1996]. "Limited attention" models provide a way to explain these phenomena and to impose some structure on the behavioral assumptions needed to generate them.

A common feature of the limited attention models is that some investors have incomplete information.[8] For example, in Hirshleifer and Teoh [2003] and Hirshleifer et al. [2011a,b], investors are assumed to have mean–variance preferences and are identical expect that some are inattentive and form their beliefs using only a subset of all information. Note that while investor inattention is typically modeled as an omission of information signals, it can also be modeled as the use of heuristics or simplified models when forming expectations. The key in each case is that some information is overlooked by a subset of investors, and this information fails to become incorporated into price. See Lim and Teoh [2010] for a good review of the literature.

Limited attention models offer a general framework for understanding market-pricing anomalies. In this framework, various fundamental

---

[8]The earliest version is Merton [1987], who refers to his as an "incomplete information model." Merton does not appeal to cognitive constraints, but some of the investors in his model possess incomplete information and behave much like the inattentive investors in later models. Other examples include: Hirshleifer and Teoh [2003], Sims [2003], Peng and Xiong [2006]; and Hirshleifer et al. [2011a].

signals predict future returns because a subset of investors do not fully recognize the information that is contained in the signal. To the extent that a particular piece of information (such as the implication of recent earnings surprises for future earnings in Bernard and Thomas, 1990; or the lower persistence of accruals relative to cash flows in Sloan, 1996) is ignored by the inattentive investors, this information will prove useful in predicting future returns.

When investors have limited attention, the degree to which a piece of information is incorporated into price will depend on both the saliency of the information and the presence of other distractions. Consistent with this hypothesis, Della Vigna and Pollet [2009] report more muted immediate market reactions to Friday earnings announcements, followed by stronger drifts. Francis et al. [1992] and Bagnoli et al. [2005] find a greater underreaction to earnings news released during non-trading hours. Hirshleifer et al. [2009] find that when an earnings announcement is made on days with many competing announcements, the immediate price reaction is weaker, and the post-announcement drift stronger. Finally, Drake et al. [2015] find that the market response to earnings news released during the NCAA basketball tournament (March Madness) is also more muted, and less likely to be fully incorporated into price immediately. In each case, investor distractions seem to affect the speed and efficacy of the market response to earnings news.

Barber and Odean [BO, 2008] show that individual investors are particularly prone to "attention-driven buying". Specifically, they find retail investors are net buyers of attention-grabbing stocks — that is, stocks in the news, or experiencing abnormal trading volume and/or extreme returns. They attribute this finding to the fact that retail investors do not face the same search problem when selling because they tend to sell only stocks they already own. The BO result establishes the importance of search costs, at least in the case of retail investors. At the same time, BO suggests that attention-grabbing stocks may be particularly susceptible to overvaluation, as retail investors bid their prices upward relative to fundamentals.

Da et al. [DEG, 2011] use the search frequency in Google ("Search Volume Index" or SVI) to develop a direct measure of investor attention. Applying this firm-specific measure to a sample of Russell 3000 stocks, they show that SVI is a useful measure of investor attention. Consistent with the price pressure hypothesis in BO, they find that an increase in SVI predicts higher stock prices in the next two weeks, and an eventual price reversal within the year. They also provide some evidence that SVI is related to the large first-day return and long-run underperformance of IPO stocks.

Engelberg et al. [ESW, 2012b] use the popular television show Mad Money, hosted by Jim Cramer, to test theories of attention and limits to arbitrage. They find that stock recommendations on Mad Money lead to large overnight returns that subsequently reverse over the next few months. Using daily Nielsen ratings as a direct measure of attention, they find that the overnight return is strongest when high-income viewership is high. Consistent with the BO observation that retail investors can only sell what they own, ESW finds only a weak price effect among Cramer's sell recommendations.

Taken together, the evidence in DEG and ESW supports the retail attention hypothesis of Barber and Odean [2008] and illustrates the potential role of media in generating mispricing. When search costs are high, events that focus retail investor attention on a stock tend to lead to overvaluation, followed by subsequent return reversals.

5.3.2 Task complexity

Closely related to Limited Attention is the notion of Task Complexity. As Kahneman [1973] observed, attention takes effort. The same can be said for performing complicated tasks. Some types of information are simply subtler, and more difficult to decipher from the data. Academic evidence shows that this type of information seems to diffuse more slowly into market prices.

Consider the case of economically linked firms. Using a dataset of firms' principal customers, Cohen and Frazzini [2008] show that stock prices of related firms adjust with a lag to new information about their trading partners. Consistent with investor inattention to customer–supplier links, the authors document a significant lead-lag return patterns across related firms. A monthly strategy of buying firms whose customers had the most positive returns (highest quintile) in the previous month, and selling short firms whose customers had the most negative returns (lowest quintile), yields abnormal returns of 1.55% per month, or an annualized return of 18.6% per year. Returns to this "customer momentum" strategy have little or no exposure to the standard traded risk factors, including the firm's own momentum in stock returns.

Menzly and Ozbas [2010] reports a similar pattern of slow information diffusion cross-related industries. Using the Benchmark Input-Output Surveys of the Bureau of Economic Analysis (BEA Surveys), the authors identify supplier and customer industries. They find that stocks in economically related supplier and customer industries cross-predict each other's returns. Trading strategies designed to exploit these patterns generate annual alphas as high as 8.7%, with the results being weaker for stocks with high levels of analyst coverage and institutional investors. Like Cohen and Frazzini, the results in Menzly and Ozbas suggest that stock prices adjust slowly to new information about economically linked firms.

Cohen and Lou [2012] use a novel research design to directly test the effect of information processing complexity on price adjustment. They define a conglomerate as a firm that spans more than one industry. For each conglomerate, they then construct a "pseudo-conglomerate" (PC) that consists of a portfolio of the conglomerate's segments made up of only standalone firms from the respective industries. As the PCs are composed of (comparatively) easy-to-analyze firms subject to the same industry shocks, the authors predict that their prices will be updated first. Consequently, the value-weighted average returns of the PC portfolio should predict the future updating of their paired conglomerate firms.

Cohen and Lou find strong evidence in support of their hypothesis. Specifically, a portfolio that goes long in those conglomerate firms whose corresponding PCs performed in the prior period and short in those conglomerate firms whose PCs performed worst, has value-weighted returns of 95 basis points in the following month. The analogous equal-weighted portfolio earns 118 basis points per month. These results are unaffected by controls for size, book-to-market, past returns, and liquidity. Moreover, there is no evidence of any future reversal, suggesting that the predictability in conglomerate firm returns is due to delayed updating of fundamental news rather than due to short-term investor sentiment.

The effect of complexity on information processing documented in Cohen and Lou is also found in a remarkable number of other studies. For example, the following studies show that market prices adjust sluggishly to: (1) Innovations whose worth can be estimated from firms' prior track record [Cohen et al., 2013a]; (2) Non-routine insider transactions [Cohen et al., 2012]; (3) The voting records of legislators whose constituents are the affected industries [Cohen et al., 2013b]; (4) Firms with well-connected board members [Larcker et al., 2013]; (5) Higher innovation analyst earnings revisions [Gleason and Lee, 2003]; (6) Intra-industry lead-lag information [Hou, 2007]; (7) Slow-moving demographic information [Della Vigna and Pollet, 2007]; and (8) the relative saliency of past price momentum measures [Da et al., 2015].

In each case, the predictive signal is based on publicly available data that required more detailed analysis and processing. In Gleason and Lee [2003] for example, market participants seem to understand the *quantity* (that is, the numeric magnitude) of analysts' earnings revisions, but fail to understand its *quality* (that is, which analyst issued the revision, and whether the revision is moving toward or away from the consensus forecast). In Cohen et al. [2012], market participants seem to have trouble in distinguishing between routine insider transactions (which are not predictive of subsequent returns) and non-routine transactions (which do predict returns). In Da et al. [2015], market participants miss the pricing implications of past return momentum that occurs *gradually*, but are able to fully price past return momentum that occurs *discretely* (or more saliently). We do not have room here to survey all the other studies in detail, however it suffices to say that a similar pattern emerges in each.

These studies support the view that signal complexity impedes the speed of market price adjustment. In each case, more subtle aspects of new signals are more likely to lead to delays in market price adjustment.

Evidently the additional complexity involved in the analysis is a contributing factor in the market's failure to decipher the significance of the information.

Another interesting set of findings come from the "recognition vs. disclosure" debate in accounting. In brief, the economic effect of a transaction can be either reported in the financial statement themselves ("recognized") or documented in the footnotes of these statements ("disclosed"). A consistent finding in this literature is that markets seem to pay more attention to items that are given recognition in the financial statements, rather than disclosed in the footnotes (see for example, Bernard and Schipper, 1994 and Schipper, 2007). If the quality of the information content is identical, it is difficult to understand why the market pays more attention to recognized items than those that are disclosed in the footnotes.

One leading explanation is that the information in the footnotes are less reliable (that is, it is relegated to the footnotes because it is of lower quality). An alternative explanation is that investors' information processing costs are higher for items disclosed in footnotes. If investors have limited attention, more salient numbers ("recognized" items) would receive more attention than less salient ones ("footnoted" items).

A number of recent findings seem to suggest that reliability differences cannot fully explain the lower weight placed on the footnoted items [Ahmed et al., 2006, Michels, 2013, Yu, 2013]. Even highly reliable fair value estimates of core assets from real-estate investment trusts appear less "price relevant" when they are disclosed in footnotes rather than recognized in the statements [Muller et al., 2015]. Perhaps task complexity and limited attention can help explain the differential market response to these footnoted items.

Task complexity has been proposed as an explanation for a number of other accounting-related pricing anomalies. For example, Richardson et al. [2005] posit that the market does not fully understand the differential reliability of various components of accounting accruals. Grouping these component elements of total accruals by their likely degree of reliability, the authors find that the mispricing associated with accruals is much larger for the less reliable (least persistent) elements. More recently, Call et al. [CHSY, 2015] develop a firm-specific estimate of the differential persistence in accruals and operating cash flows that is useful in out-of-sample forecasting of future earnings. CHSY show that a trading strategy based on their persistence measures and exploiting investors' fixation on earnings earn economically significant excess returns. In these, and what is by now a long list of other studies, task complexity appears to play a role in the speed of the price adjustment to publicly available accounting information.

5.3.3 Information uncertainty

Information uncertainty (IU) is a concept that is closely aligned with both limited attention and task complexity. Jiang et al. [2005] define IU in terms of "value ambiguity," or the degree to which a firm's value can be reasonably estimated by even the most knowledgeable investors at reasonable costs. By this definition, high-IU firms are companies whose expected cash flows are less "knowable," perhaps due to the nature of their business or operating environment. These firms are associated with higher information acquisition costs, and estimates of their fundamental values are inherently less reliable and more volatile.

Jiang et al. [2005] and Zhang [2006a] argue that IU, as defined above, provides a unifying framework for understanding a number of curious results in empirical asset-pricing. Specifically, prior studies have found that firms with higher volatility [Ang et al., 2006], higher trading volume [Lee and Swaminathan, 2000], greater expected growth [La Porta, 1996], higher price-to-book ratios [Fama and French, 1992], wider dispersion in analyst earnings forecasts [Diether et al., 2002], and longer implied duration in their future cash flows [Dechow et al., 2004], all earn lower subsequent returns. Although various explanations have been proposed for these phenomena, it is also true that in each instance, firms operating in higher IU environments are observed to earn lower future returns.

These empirical results are puzzling because in standard CAPM or multi-factor asset-pricing models, non-systematic risk is not priced, and various IU proxies should have no ability to predict returns. Some analytical models have argued in favor of a role for information risk in asset-pricing (see, for example, Easley and O'Hara [2004]), but even in these models the directional prediction is inconsistent with the IU findings. If higher IU firms are associated with *higher* information risk or greater information acquisition costs, why do they earn *lower* future returns?

Jiang et al. [2005] propose a behavioral explanation for the IU effect. Citing theoretical work in behavioral finance, Jiang et al. note that market mispricings arise when two conditions are met: (1) an uninformed demand shock ("noise trading"), and (2) a limit on rational arbitrage. Their two-part thesis is that the level of information uncertainty is positively correlated with a particular form of decision bias (investor overconfidence), and that it is also positively correlated with arbitrage costs. Collectively, these two effects conspire to produce lower mean returns among high-IU firms.

Jiang et al. [2005] argue that investor overconfidence is accentuated in high-IU settings, leading to greater underreaction to public signals such as the information contained in recent earnings or returns. In support of this hypothesis, both Jiang et al. [2005] and Zhang [2006a] show that momentum profits — returns from trading on recent earnings surprises or price movements — are much larger among high-IU firms. In a follow-up study, Zhang [2006b] shows that analyst earnings forecasts also exhibit the same underreaction to recent news as the stock returns. Since analyst earnings forecasts are not affected by firm risk or short-selling costs, the Zhang [2006b] result directly supports the notion that market participants tend to underreact to recent news in high-IU settings.

Finally, Stein [2009] discusses two other sources of information uncertainty that complicate active investing. The first is the uncertainty associated with the degree of "crowdedness" in a trade. Even the most sophisticated investors cannot always be certain how many of her peers are simultaneously entering the same trade. We have already seen in Section 3 that mutual fund trades exhibit directional "herding" at the daily level [Arif et al., 2015], but the phenomenon is more general, and applies to any trader with information that may not be fully incorporated into the current price.

A second source of information uncertainty relates to the optimal level of "leverage" to use. Individual managers may decide on a privately optimal level of leverage based on his own backtest and risk tolerance. Unfortunately these privately optimal decisions may not result in an optimal amount of leverage for the industry as a whole. When macro conditions change, if the industry is collectively over-levered, the increased likelihood of fire sales that lead to market crashes arise as an externality. Of course, it is impossible to arrive at a collectively optimal amount of leverage without some coordination, possibly involving market regulators. In this case, once again, information uncertainty leads to higher costs for rational money seeking to discipline market prices.

In sum, limited attention, task complexity, and information uncertainty can all complicate matters for smart money investors. Where these problems are more severe, we observe large and more persistent market mispricings. Viewed through the lens of the noise trader model, these three information acquisition and processing costs influence market pricing because they: (1) increase the likelihood of investor errors, and (2) reduce the ease with which these errors can be identified and arbitraged away by rational investors.

5.4 Implementation and execution costs

Transaction and execution costs serve as important constraints that limit rational arbitrage. Most academic asset-pricing studies focus on gross returns to assets without considering transaction costs. However, the professional arbitrageur's decisions are based on expected profits, net of the costs associated with trade execution and strategy implementation. Therefore, one possible explanation for the continued existence of many predictive patterns reported in academic studies is that the costs of exploiting them are prohibitive.

5.4.1 Trading costs

The most common trading costs include:

1. Fees and commissions (generally paid to brokers; the stock exchanges in some countries also impose "stamp duties" or "transaction fees");

2. The bid–ask spread (the difference between the asking price and the offer price); and,

3. The price impact cost (also called "price slippage", it is the amount by which price moves as the order is being executed).

Estimates for commissions, fees, and bid–ask spreads are relatively easy to obtain, but for professional asset managers, they are less important than the price impact cost. The bid–ask spread is of little consequence to a professional asset manager because it only reflects the round trip cost for trading a small number of shares. For these investors, transaction cost management involves minimizing the *total cost* of filling an order, which is often quite large. Typically, most of this cost will come from the price impact that the order has on the security.

In general, the price impact of an order to buy or sell a security will depend on: (1) The size of the order, (2) The average daily volume (ADV) of the security, and (3) The urgency with which it must be filled (which in turn may depend on the type of investment strategy being deployed). Orders that are "large" relative to ADV (say an order to buy or sell a position that is 5% or more of average daily volume) will likely experience substantial price slippage. In addition, aggressive orders that demand immediate execution (common to "trend-chasing" or "momentum" strategies) will incur greater price slippage than patient orders that provide liquidity to others (common to "contrarian" strategies).

In their classic study on execution costs for institutional equity trades, Keim and Madhavan [KM, 1997, p. 275] report that the average total cost of an institutional buy order is 0.49% and the cost of an average sell order is 0.55% for NYSE/AMEX listed stocks. The average total cost for buy (sell) orders on the Nasdaq is 1.23% (1.43%), suggesting a total round-trip cost of approximately 1% to 2.6%. Trading costs have declined sharply over the years since the KM study was done. In a more recent study, Engle et al. [2012] estimate average one-way transaction costs for professional traders to be around 9 basis points for NYSE stocks and 14 basis points for NASDAQ stocks, based on actual orders executed by Morgan Stanley in 2004. In other words, round-trip trading costs for these particular transactions were in the order of 0.18% to 0.28%, which is certainly much lower than the costs 10 years earlier.

In a more recent study, Frazzini et al. [FIM, 2012] examine the actual trading costs incurred by a large institutional asset manager trading in 19 stock exchanges in developed countries over the 1998–2011 period. Using nearly one trillion dollars of live trading data, they measured the execution costs and price impact associated with trades based on value, size, momentum, and price-reversal strategies. Instead of reporting round-trip transaction costs, FIM report the "break-even" capacity of each type of strategy. In other words, they estimate how much money can be managed globally using each of the four strategies before the strategy earns zero-profit after trading costs. They report that value, size, momentum, and price-reversal strategies applied globally generate break-even sizes of 1,807, 811, 122, and 17 billion dollars, respectively. In other words, a value strategy running roughly 1.8 trillion dollars would result in zero profits after transaction costs. Based on this analysis, they conclude that the "main anomalies to standard asset-pricing models are robust, implementable, and sizeable."

Aside from the three direct trading costs discussed above, asset managers often incur other implementation and execution expenses, include: (1) Hedging costs, which reflect the cost of taking an offsetting position in a hedging asset, if relevant; (2) Holding costs (sometimes called "the carry", which reflects the cost of keeping both positions open for the anticipated period needed for price convergence, including the financing cost if these trades involves leverage); and (3) Short-sale costs, which reflect costs of borrowing a security you do not own in order to take on a short-position).

Hedging and holding costs can vary widely by strategy and are beyond the scope of this section. In the next subsection we will focus on a more common cost of particular relevant to active equity investors; specifically, the cost of short-selling a stock.

5.4.2   Short-sale constraints

One aspect of equity markets that has received increased academic attention in recent years is the informational role played by short sellers.

Academic studies have consistently demonstrated that, as a group, short-sellers are sophisticated investors with superior information processing capabilities (see, for example, Dechow et al. [2001], Desai et al. [2002], Drake et al. [2011], and Engelberg et al. [2012a]). At the intraday level, short-sale flows improve the informational efficiency of intraday prices [Boehmer and Wu, 2013]. Globally, the introduction of short-selling in international markets is associated with a lowering of country-level costs-of-capital, an increase in market liquidity, and an improvement in overall pricing efficiency [Daouk et al., 2006, Bris et al., 2007].

Given the importance of short-sellers to informational arbitrage, it is not surprising that short-selling constraints directly affect market-pricing efficiency. Numerous studies have linked short-sale constraints to stock overvaluation (see, for example, Asquith et al. [2005], Geczy et al. [2002], Jones and Lamont [2002], Ljungqvist and Qian [2014], and Beneish et al. [2015]). Even temporary short-selling bans appear to impede pricing efficiency in the banned stocks [Battalio and Schultz, 2011, Boehmer et al., 2012].

A particularly serious constraint to rational arbitrage is the availability of lendable shares and the costs associated with locating them [Beneish et al., 2015]. Although average daily open short interest in the U.S. now exceeds 1.0 trillion dollars, equity loan transactions are still conducted in an archaic over-the-counter (OTC) market. In this market, borrowers (typically hedge funds) must first contact prime brokers, who in turn "locate" (that is, check on the availability of) the requisite shares, often by consulting multiple end lenders.[9] In the absence of a centralized market clearing mechanism, it is difficult for participants in the equity loan market to secure an overarching view of real-time conditions. The problem is exacerbated in foreign markets, particularly in countries (such as China and India) with limited supplies of lendable shares.

Our main point is that informational efficiency in the stock market is inextricably linked to informational efficiency in the market for

---

[9]Total open short interest is reported monthly by NYSE and twice per month by NASDAQ. See D'Avolio [2002], Fabozzi [2004], Kolasinski et al. [2013], and Beneish et al. [2015] for good summaries of institutional details on equity loan markets.

equity loans.[10] When constraints in the market for equity loans are binding, these constraints invariably hinder the pricing efficiency of the underlying stocks.

5.5 Funding and financing constraints

5.5.1 Access to arbitrage capital

Like any business, professional asset managers need to raise and retain capital. To do so, they need the continuous support of their investors. This support is particularly important when a strategy is underperforming. Unfortunately, this support is also much harder to come by during such times. As a result, asset managers often run into financing constraints precisely when the differential between price and value is most extreme, and arbitrage capital is most needed [Shleifer and Vishny, 1997]. The existence of these financing constraints is another important reason why arbitrage mechanisms do not eliminate mispricing.

As discussed in Section 3 on Investor Sentiment, capital flows into many asset categories exhibit uncannily bad timing ability. The heaviest investor inflows into equity markets typically portend market tops, and the heaviest outflows typically portend market bottoms [Dichev, 2007, Baker et al., 2012, Ben-Rephael et al., 2012, Arif and Lee, 2015]. These inflow and outflow patterns also apply to individual hedge funds [Dichev and Yu, 2011]. In all these cases, investors take money out of underperforming strategies or asset classes, and redeploy this capital in other ways. Unfortunately for them, more often than not, these money flows seem to take place precisely when the strategy or asset class is about to experience a reversal in fortune.

To be fair, it is not easy to settle on the right asset manager (or the right asset allocation mix). When prices are noisy, a long period of time may be needed to separate the skillful managers from the lucky ones [Grinold and Kahn, 1999]. Given sufficient heterogeneity across money managers, discriminating between them can be difficult. In

---

[10]Blocher et al. [BRVW, 2013] formally models the two markets as a joint equilibrium.

fact, Berk and Green [2004] show that when managerial ability must be inferred from past performance, it may be rational for capital flows to chase performance, even though the performance itself is not persistent.

Of course, it is one thing to understand the problem, and quite another to overcome it. In models without agency problems, arbitrageurs are generally more aggressive when prices move further from fundamental values [see Grossman and Miller, 1988, DeLong et al., 1990a, Campbell and Kyle, 1993]. In these models, capital constraints are unimportant because arbitrage is conducted by multiple investors each with a small amount of funds. However, as Shleifer and Vishny [1997] observed, real-world arbitrage typically involves a smaller set of professional investors pursuing highly specialized strategies while managing other people's money. In these settings, capital constraints can be most binding when price is furthest from fundamental value, and arbitrage capital can dry up precisely when it is most needed to discipline widespread mispricing.

Brunnermeier and Nagel [BN, 2004] offer some empirical support for the SV prediction. BN examine hedge fund behavior during the two years leading up to the March 2000 technology bubble. During this extreme period of overvaluation for technology stocks, BN show that hedge fund managers did not exert a correcting force on stock prices. Instead they were heavily invested in technology stocks, although many managed to reduce their positions in time to avoid much of the downturn. Fund managers who stayed the course and avoided technology investments generally fared poorly. In fact, BN show that the manager with the least exposure to technology stocks — Tiger Management — did not manage to survive until the bubble burst.

A recent study by Hanson and Sunderam [2014] offers further support for SV's limits-to-arbitrage argument. In this study, the authors use short interest data to infer the amount of capital allocated to quantitative equity arbitrage strategies. They find that the amount of capital devoted to value and momentum strategies has grown significantly since the late 1980s, and that this increase in capital has resulted in lower strategy returns. More importantly, consistent with SV, they show that this arbitrage capital is most limited during times when these strategies perform best.

5.5.2 Market-wide liquidity constraints

In the wake of the 2007–2008 global financial crises, a number of academic studies have emerged that shed new light on the importance of market-wide liquidity constraints. For example, He and Krishnamurthy [HK, 2013] model the dynamics of risk premiums during crises in asset markets where the marginal investor is a financial intermediary. In their model, intermediaries face an equity capital constraint. When financial intermediaries' capital is scarce, risk premiums rise. In the same spirit, Brunnermeier and Pedersen [BP, 2009] present a model that links an asset's market liquidity (that is, the ease with which it is traded) and traders' funding liquidity (that is, the ease with which they can obtain funding). In their model, traders provide market liquidity and their ability to do so depends on their availability of funding. Conversely, traders' funding (including their capital and margin requirements) depends on the assets' market liquidity.

An especially interesting feature in BP is the occurrence of "liquidity spirals." BP show that under certain conditions, capital margin requirements can be destabilizing and market liquidity and funding liquidity can become mutually reinforcing. In these states of the world, market liquidity can suddenly dry up, with implications for security prices, overall market volatility, "flights to quality", and price co-movements across assets whose returns are normally uncorrelated. In their model, all results derive because when speculators' capital becomes constrained, it has predictable consequences for market liquidity and risk premiums.

The idea of liquidity crashes is also prominent in Cespa and Foucault [2014]. In their model, the liquidity of a security is closely related to the amount of information its price coveys to traders about its true worth. When an exogenous liquidity shock occurs in security Y, its price becomes less informative, thus increasing uncertainty for dealers, some of whom also trade a different security (security X). This second security then experiences a drop in liquidity that decreases the information its price conveys about security Y, leading to a further decline in the liquidity of Y, and so forth. Like BP, the authors nominate liquidity constraints as a source of fragility in market prices.

The empirical results in Nyborg and Ostberg [NO, 2014] are broadly consistent with these models. NO argue that tightness in the market for liquidity leads banks to engage in "liquidity pull-backs," which involve the selling of financial assets either by banks directly or by levered investors. In support of this hypothesis, they show that tighter inter-bank markets (measured using the three-month Libor-OIS spread)[11] are associated with relatively higher trading volume in more liquid stocks; increased selling pressure in general; and transitory negative returns.

Along the same vein, Hu et al. [HPW, 2013] study the impact of market-wide funding constraints on U.S. Treasury yields. Specifically, HPW note that the smoothness in the U.S. Treasury Bond yield curve is attributable to professional arbitrageurs, whose activities ensure that bonds of similar durations offer similar yields. Therefore, deviations of bond prices from a smooth yield curve (referred to as "noise") are indicative of a lack of arbitrage capital. During "noisy" periods, arbitrageurs lack sufficient ability or willingness to deploy the capital necessary to push bond prices toward fundamental value.

HPW find that the availability of arbitrage capital fluctuates over time in response to macroeconomic conditions. For example, their noise measure falls during periods of government surpluses and reductions in the gross issuance of U.S. Treasury securities. During these periods of ample capital, the average deviation of the Treasury yield from a smooth curve falls well within the securities' bid–ask spreads. Conversely, during market-wide liquidity crises (such as the October 1987 crash, the collapse of Long-Term Capital Management (LTCM), and the Lehman default), U.S. Treasury securities of similar durations can trade at wildly different yields, suggesting serious price misalignments. Moreover, during these periods of capital scarcity, HPW show that their noise measure often exceeded bid–ask spreads, indicating trading opportunities that went unexploited.

---

[11]Libor is London Interbank Offered Rate, OIS is overnight index swap. The difference between these two rates is a general measure of tightness in the interbank market (that is, it is a measure of the price banks charge each other for overnight liquidity). The authors also run their tests using the TED spread (that is, the three-month Libor less the three-month Treasury bill rate) and find similar results.

In sum, both theoretical and empirical evidence suggest that market-wide funding constraints can impact pricing efficiency. Funding constraints of this nature can limit price discovery through several channels including, but not limited to, reductions in lending, declining collateral needed for leverage, and increases in cash reserves to meet investor redemptions.

5.5.3   Funding constraints and asset prices

Do the funding constraints of arbitrageurs help explain pricing behavior across large groups of assets? Yes, as it turns out, tightness in the market for arbitrage capital can have a dramatic effect on the cross-section of asset prices. In fact, returns on assets that have little or no obvious fundamental links appear to co-move strongly in response to ebbs and flows in the supply of arbitrage capital.

Some of the most compelling evidence comes from a recent study by Adrian et al. [AEM, 2014]. AEM begin by noting that asset prices should be determined by their covariances with a stochastic discount factor (SDF), which is usually linked to the margin value of aggregate wealth. The idea is that assets which are expected to pay off in future states with high marginal value of wealth (think "recessions") are worth more today. Much of the empirical asset-pricing literature has focused on measuring the marginal value of wealth for a representative investor, typically by aggregating wealth over all households.

In a novel twist, AEM shift attention from measuring the SDF of the average household to measuring what they call a "financial intermediary SDF." Inspired by some of the models above, AEM argue that if we can measure the marginal value of wealth for active investors, we can expect to price a broad class of assets. AEM then use the leverage of security broker-dealers as an empirical proxy for the marginal value of wealth of financial intermediaries. Intuitively, when funding conditions tighten and intermediaries are forced to deleverage, their marginal value of wealth would be high.

The empirical findings in AEM strongly support this line of reasoning. Using shocks to the leverage of securities broker-dealers, the construct an "intermediary SDF." Remarkably, they find that this *single*-factor model prices size, book-to-market, momentum, and bond portfolios with an R-squared of 77% and an average annual pricing error of 1%. In other words, a single factor based on shocks to funding conditions among broker-dealers outperforms standard multifactor model tailored to price these cross-sections, including the Fama and French [1993] three-factor model and the five-factor Carhart [1997] model that includes a momentum factor and a bond-pricing factor.

Discussing their results, AEM note that they support a growing theoretical literature on links between financial institutions and asset prices. They write:

> Most directly, our results support models in which leverage captures the time-varying balance sheet capacity of financial intermediaries. As funding constraints tighten, balance sheet capacity falls and intermediaries are forced to deleverage by selling assets at fire sale prices, as in the recent financial crisis ... assets that pay off poorly when constraints tighten and leverage falls are therefore risky and must offer high returns. [Adrian et al., 2014, p. 2560].

In case you missed this, what AEM are saying is that active fund managers who invest using strategies based on firm size, book-to-market, momentum, and bonds, all face a common stochastic risk. These strategies that are prevalent among hedge funds all earn higher expected returns over normal time periods. However, they will all lose money when broker-dealers suddenly experience a tightening in their funding conditions.

Allow us to reframe these latest results from the empirical asset-pricing literature within the context of this research monograph. One way to interpret these results is that the average excess returns earned by many of these characteristic-based portfolios are real. In fact, professional arbitrageurs routinely exploit these patterns. However, betting on these patterns can be risky, because arbitrage capital is constrained. From time-to-time, when this capital is withdrawn, these strategies will underperform.

Summary

Despite their importance, arbitrage costs are far less understood and appreciated in academia than in practice. Many academics find it difficult to understand why a flood of smart money does not immediately rush forth to extinguish mispricings as soon as they appear. This section surveys the current state of the literature on limits-to-arbitrage and seeks to explain to an academic audience some of the practical challenges faced by professional fund managers who shape price discovery within financial markets.

As the studies surveyed here show, smart money seeking to conduct rational informational arbitrage faces many costs and challenges. These challenges can dramatically limit the deployment of arbitrage capital in financial markets, leading to significant price dislocations. Such effects are pervasive across asset groups, and have important pricing implications even in the most liquid financial markets. It is difficult to see how a belief in market efficiency and unconstrained arbitrage can be sustained in the face of such compelling evidence to the contrary.

We organized our discussion around three broad categories of arbitrage costs and constraints, associated with: (1) identifying/verifying the mispricing, (2) implementing/executing the strategy, and (3) financing/funding the business. Much of the literature on limits-to-arbitrage has focused on the second and third categories — that is, implementation/execution costs and financing/funding constraints. Although these constraints are important, we believe the first category — that is, the costs and risks associated with identifying and verifying the mispricing — is also deserving of more academic attention. On this point, we find recent advances on the role of limited investor attention and task complexity particularly promising.

Our central message is that real-world arbitrage is an information game that involves a constantly improving technology. Asset managers face substantial uncertainty and risk whenever they try to identify/verify, finance/fund, and execute/implement an active strategy.

At every stage of this process, they need better (more precise; more reliable) information. The right kind of information can help asset managers to identify mispricing, reduce risk, secure funding, and improve trade execution. Our hope and expectation is that academics will play an important role in bringing this kind of information to light.

6

Research Methodology: Predictability in Asset Returns

Evidence of predictable returns is often met with controversy. This controversy stems from an inherent conflict between tenets of market efficiency and securities analysis. More extreme forms of market efficiency argue that prices immediately and consistently incorporate all available information and, thus, that any predictable returns must reflect compensation for risk, even if the source of the risk is not readily identifiable [Fama, 1970]. On the opposite end of the spectrum, a central premise of security analysis is that sophisticated investors can use publicly available information to identify and implement profitable investment strategies. The stark contrast between these views has motivated researchers and practitioners to develop a wide array of techniques useful in understanding the sources of predictable asset returns. In this section, we survey techniques useful in adjudicating between risk and mispricing explanations for predictability in asset returns.

The motivation for this section is academic as well as practical. Both academics and investors who observe predictability patterns in returns are motivated to understand the reason for their existence. Investors have an inherent interest in distinguishing between returns that stem from mispricing versus exposure to risk, because the relative

153

magnitudes of these two components ultimately define the attractiveness of investment opportunities. Whereas mispricing implies abnormal profit opportunities that might be further exploited, risk-based explanations imply that the returns are earned at the expense of safety, and are thus accompanied by a higher likelihood of adverse outcomes.

From an academic perspective, studies that identify a predictable pattern in future returns alone face an uphill battle to satisfy the minimum standards required for a top-tier publication. In the absence of a plausible explanation for the findings, or at least some underpinning intuition, statistical patterns of abnormal return are likely to be treated with skepticism. Even if they are published, such findings typically only have widespread impact if later research establishes an economic or psychological foundation for the finding (see Section 6.10 for further discussion of assessing incremental contribution).

To further complicate matters, risk- and mispricing-based explanations for return predictability are not mutually exclusive. In many instances, assets with higher expected returns do indeed have higher exposure to certain risk factors. These issues raise a number of questions for both researchers and practitioners: What is the right standard for assessing whether a research result is due to risk or mispricing? What types of evidence should we expect researchers, particularly academics, to deliver? This section addresses these questions and offers suggestions for future research.

6.1 Exposure to risk factors

Risk-based explanations for return predictability are rooted in the idea that riskier assets have higher expected returns than less risky assets. The higher expected return reflects equilibrium compensation that investors receive for holding assets with greater potential to create adverse wealth shocks. Guided by this fundamental concept, researchers attempt to distinguish risk and mispricing explanations for return predictability by comparing realized returns with measures of the asset's expected return. Systematic deviations between realized and expected returns then serve as a starting point for tests of market inefficiencies.

One of the most common representations of expected returns is in terms of a linear factor-pricing model such as the Capital Asset Pricing Model (CAPM) or Arbitrage Pricing Theory (APT). In these classic asset-pricing models, an asset's expected returns are a compensation for its exposure, or sensitivity, to market-wide "factors" that characterize the state of the economy. As discussed in Cochrane [2011], a linear asset-pricing model implies that the expected return for an asset with exposure to Z factors will take the following form:

$$E[R_{i,t}] = \gamma + \beta_{i,a}\lambda_a + \beta_{i,b}\lambda_b + \cdots + \beta_{i,z}\lambda_z \qquad (6.1)$$

The above representation shows that a security's expected returns are determined by two components. The β component of expected returns denotes an asset's sensitivity to a given risk factor. As the sensitivity of a given asset to common risk factors increases, investors are expected to demand greater risk premiums because the investor faces greater exposure to these sources of risk.

The λ component indicates the equilibrium compensation earned for exposure to a given risk factor. Commonly referred to as factor returns, λ measures the premiums investors demand for exposure to various dimensions of non-diversifiable risk. In the case of the CAPM, investors accept negative expected returns on assets that perform well when the market declines (that is, have a negative market beta), presumably because the marginal utility for wealth is highest in times of macroeconomic distress when the market portfolio declines in value. As noted in Equation (1), an asset's expected return equals the total amount of risk as indicated by the asset's sensitivity, β, multiplied by the per-unit compensation for exposure to non-diversifiable risk, λ.

In the context of linear factor-pricing models, abnormal returns refer to any systematic difference between an asset's realized returns and its expected returns. Empirically, once a researcher has decided on a set of factors to include in the estimate of expected returns, she may estimate a security's β's by calculating the coefficients in the following time-series regression of historical returns on historical factor returns:

$$R_{i,t} = \alpha + \beta_{i,a} f_{t,a} + \beta_{i,b} f_{t,b} + \cdots + \beta_{i,z} f_{t,z} + \varepsilon \qquad (6.2)$$

where f are empirical proxies for risk factor premiums. Common empirical proxies for these premiums include the excess return to the market portfolio, as well as the return on various "factor mimicking" portfolios formed by sorting firms on various ex ante characteristics.

For example, in Fama and French [1993], the factor portfolios are the excess return on the market (MKT), the return differential between small and large firms (SMB) and the return differential between high- and low- book-to-market firms (HML). The intercept term in this regression is the "abnormal" return to the security (or portfolio). Another variation in this approach made popular by Carhart [1997] adds a price momentum factor, defined as the return differential between a portfolio of past "winner" firms and past "losers", commonly referred to as UMD (short for up-minus-down). To the extent that these regressions succeed in removing the component of realized returns attributable to an asset's exposure to the factors, the resulting abnormal returns are more likely to indicate mispricing.

Close analogues to the factor-based approach are the *characteristic-based* tests that examine whether a given signal can predict returns over-and-above a set of other firm characteristics (see, for example, Fama and French [1992]). In this approach, the researcher conducts a series of cross-sectional regressions at various points in time (for example, typically at monthly, quarterly, or annual intervals). The dependent variable in each regression is the future returns of a firm. The independent variables include a candidate signal and a set of firm-level control variables that are presumed to control for cross-sectional variation in risk. Common nominees include firm size, book-to-market, and return momentum. If the candidate signal predicts returns incremental to these control variables, the evidence of return predictability is interpreted as being less likely to reflect risk.

The factor-based tests [Fama and French, 1993, Carhart, 1997] and the characteristic-based tests [Fama and French, 1992] have become mainstays in studies of realized security returns.[1] An important appeal of these approaches is their link to asset-pricing theory. The factors in these models are intended to represent systemic (market-wide and thus undiversifiable) sources of risk. Asset-pricing theory suggests that, in equilibrium, only undiversifiable risk (that is, a firm's betas, or its loadings, on these individual factors) should be priced. Therefore a security's risk-based expected returns should be a function of its sensitivity to these factors.

Another appealing feature of these models is that they are quite general. Although factor-based models are commonly used to explain equity market returns, they also apply to other financial assets, such as bonds. As noted in Fama and French [1993], to the extent that markets are integrated across asset classes, a single model should also explain the returns of these assets. This single-model perspective opens up the possibility of testing for market inefficiencies in markets other than equities.

From an investor's perspective, these approaches also have a certain pragmatic appeal. Even if one is agnostic on whether the returns to the factor portfolios returns represent risk or mispricing, it is still helpful to know how much of a security (or a portfolio's) realized returns are orthogonal to the returns on a set of factor-mimicking portfolios. This would be useful, for example, when an investor is calibrating the incremental predictive power of a new signal relative to a set of existing factors. Similarly, the characteristic-based tests provide information about the incremental usefulness of a new signal in returns prediction relative to other known predictors of returns.

It is important to recognize that these tests are also subject to some serious shortcomings. The central problem is related to model misspecification [Fama, 1991]. These asset-pricing tests are designed to identify variation in realized returns that are orthogonal to the chosen set of factors. To the extent that the underlying risk model is misspecified, these tests will fail to adjudicate between risk and mispricing.

---

[1]See, for example, Fama and French [1997], Elton [1999], and Pastor and Stambaugh [1999].

Unfortunately, asset-pricing theory offers little guidance on what else, beyond the market portfolio itself, should be included in the models.

To make matters worse, the most commonly used factors have little support in asset-pricing theory. For example, two of the most common factors are price momentum [UMD from Carhart, 1997] and book-to-market [HML from Fama and French, 1993], neither of which maps well into specific macroeconomic risks nominated by equilibrium asset-pricing theory. Of course, to the extent these factors are themselves indicators of mispricing rather than systemic risk, the factor-based tests will over-attribute realized returns to risk-based explanations.

In sum, the most commonly used risk-adjustment models have their root in equilibrium asset-pricing theory. However, the ability of these tests to adjudicate between risk and mispricing depends critically on the appropriateness of the underlying risk model. If the asset-pricing model is misspecified, researchers will not be able to reject the null hypothesis that return predictability is due to an unspecified and/or unobservable risk factor. Unfortunately the most common factors used in the literature tend to be "empirically-inspired." That is, they are factors or firm characteristics identified by prior empirical research as predictors of return, rather than factors nominated by equilibrium asset-pricing theory. Therefore, while these tests have become a staple in empirical asset-pricing, the extent to which they can truly distinguish between risk and mispricing is open to question.

So else might researchers do to distinguish between risk and mispricing? In the sections below, we motivate and detail a number of alternative approaches that can help to supplement factor-based tests in understanding the sources of predictable variation in security returns.

6.2 If it looks like risk. . .

A useful starting point when attempting to distinguish between risk and mispricing is with a thought experiment. Begin by assuming that all return predictability is driven by risk, and then ask: what type(s) of risk might plausible give rise to the observed pattern in returns? In other words, what would the risk need to look like and how would it have to operate in order to give rise the observed returns? Often, risk-based explanations seem to fail what we call the "common sense" test.

To illustrate, consider the evidence of post-earnings announcement drift (PEAD), which shows that the returns of firms with more positive earnings news tend to outperform the market after their earnings announcement and firms with more negative earnings news tend to underperform the market. The PEAD literature also shows that the price drift is more pronounced in the short-leg of the strategy among firms with negative earnings news. In order for PEAD to be driven by risk, it must be that firms become riskier when announcing positive news and less risky when announcing negative news. Moreover, risk-based explanations would need to explain why earnings news gives rise to a negative risk premium in order to explain why returns are concentrated in the short-leg of the PEAD strategy. Precisely characterizing the nature of the observed returns (for example, *when* and *where* return predictability is concentrated) not only helps to distinguish risk and mispricing but also helps researchers in understanding the role of market frictions in driving strategy returns (discussed more below).

Along the same vein, consider the evidence in Dichev [1998] and Piotroski [2000], which shows that firms with stronger accounting fundamentals (that is, healthier firms) significantly outperform firms with weaker accounting fundamentals (that is, weaker firms). Healthier firms not only earn superior stock returns but also subsequently report better earnings news than weaker firms. To explain the return patterns in these studies, it would have to be that healthier firms, measured in multiple ways, are somehow riskier than weaker firms. Thus, risk-based explanations would have to explain why risk-averse investors prefer to hold firms with weaker fundamentals and lower subsequent earnings.

More recently, researchers have developed other tests that appeal to the "common sense" criterion. For example, Ohlson and Bilinski [2015] argue that riskier stocks should experience more extreme jumps in price, both positive and negative jumps, than safer stocks, because risk should be correlated with greater uncertainty regarding the asset's future performance. Conversely, signals of mispricing should exhibit an opposite trait: that is, they should result in strategies which generate higher returns without exposing investors to an increased risk of adverse wealth shocks. Using this approach, Ohlson and Bilinski [2015] conclude that the accrual anomaly is unlikely to reflect equilibrium compensation for exposure to risk.

Daniel and Titman [1997] and Hirshleifer et al. [2012] appeal to a prediction from classical asset-pricing models to distinguish risk versus mispricing. According to standard asset-pricing theory, the ability of a signal to predict returns should be related to its suitability as an empirical proxy for an asset's sensitivity (that is, loadings) to various risk factors. Therefore, an asset's Beta (that is, loading) to a factor-mimicking portfolio constructed from the underlying signal should predict returns better than the underlying signal itself. Contrary to this prediction, Daniel and Titman [1997], Daniel et al. [1997] find that a firm's book-to-market ratio is a much better predictor of future returns than its factor loading on the HML factor portfolio. In the same spirit, Hirshleifer et al. [2012] apply this notion to accruals and show that firms' accruals, rather than their sensitivity to an accrual factor-mimicking portfolio, predict future returns. Similarly, Momente *et al.* [2015] decompose accruals into firm-specific versus related-firm components and, that contrary to asset-pricing theory, show that only the firm-specific component predicts returns. These findings cast doubt on risk-based explanations for the accrual anomaly and is more consistent with investors mispricing the implications of accruals for future cash flows.

While these common sense tests cannot completely rule out nor confirm risk-based explanations, they can guide researchers in understanding what types of risk are potentially relevant to the strategy. In each case, the researcher begins by taking the risk explanation seriously, then formulates additional tests that should hold if the phenomenon is attributable to risk. The evidence from these additional tests contributes to a "weight of evidence" argument either in favor of, or contrary to, a risk-based explanation.

6.3   Short-window returns

A common goal of academic research in accounting is to identify earnings information that is not reflected in security prices in a timely fashion. Through careful analysis of historical financial data, researchers attempt to identify overvalued and undervalued securities. Trading opportunities are present when prices do not accurately reflect the future cash flow implications of historical information in a timely manner, resulting in prices that temporarily depart from fundamental value. These price dislocations are corrected over time as future news about earnings is released.

Given the potential role of future news releases in correcting biased expectations, many studies attempt to distinguish risk and mispricing explanations by examining the returns to around subsequent earnings announcements. As least as far back as Bernard and Thomas [1990], researchers have noted that investor underreaction or overreaction to firm fundamentals should be resolved around information events that reduce uncertainty about fundamentals. Thus, the case for mispricing is strengthened if the returns to a given strategy are concentrated around subsequent earnings announcements.

Another reason for short-window tests is that the model misspecification problem is unlikely to be a significant issue when asset returns are measured over two or three day intervals. As noted in Lee and Swaminathan [2000], cross-sectional differences in expected returns are relatively small over short windows around earnings news releases. Therefore, a strategy that pays off disproportionally during subsequent earnings announcement periods is more likely to reflect the correction of biased investor expectations regarding firms' future earnings.[2]

Bernard and Thomas [1990] provide an excellent example of how researchers can use returns during earnings announcements to distinguish risk and mispricing explanations for post-earnings announcement drift (PEAD). The authors argue that PEAD stems from investor underreaction to the implications of current earnings news for future earnings. Specifically, the authors show that there is positive serial correlation in earnings surprises such that firms with positive earnings

---

[2]Kolari and Pynnönen [2010] note, however, that clustering of earnings announcements can lead to over-rejection of the null hypothesis of zero abnormal returns, particularly when the sign and magnitude of news is correlated across the announcements. We return to the issue of significance testing in the discussion below.

news tend to have additional positive earnings news at subsequent earnings announcements. To the extent that investors misprice the implications of current earnings for future earnings, such mispricing should be resolved when uncertainty over future earnings is reduced through subsequent earnings announcements. Consistent with a mispricing-based explanation for their findings, Bernard and Thomas [1990] show that a significant portion of PEAD strategy returns are realized during earnings announcements and that these returns are concentrated among firms with predictable earnings news, which together suggest that investors misprice the future earnings implications of recent earnings surprises.

Sloan [1996] provides a similar excellent example of how earnings announcement returns can be used to discern risk and mispricing explanations for accrual-based trading strategies. Sloan [1996] argues that investors underreact to the accrual component of earnings, failing to recognize that firms with a high accrual component are less likely to have persistent earnings and are more likely to underperform in the future. Sloan shows that firms with high accruals tend to underperform low accrual firms by approximately 10% per year. However, Sloan shows that approximately 40% of the annualized strategy return is realized during firms' subsequent quarterly announcement dates. The concentration of the strategy returns during the announcement suggests that investors correct biased expectations regarding the valuation implications of accruals once investors learn that past accruals have failed to materialize into net income in subsequent periods.

6.4   Other non-return-based metrics

Disagreements about whether return predictability reflects risk versus mispricing are often difficult to resolve using only realized returns and risk proxies. This is because return predictability can be attributed to risk, even if the source of risk is not directly identifiable or measurable. An alternative way to distinguish between these explanations is to examine whether a given signal is correlated with proxies for revisions in investors' expectations that do not rely on market prices.

For example, researchers commonly examine whether a signal predicts revisions in sell-side analysts' earnings forecasts or buy–sell recommendations under the assumption that analysts' forecasts and recommendations proxy for investors' expectations of a firm's performance (see, for example, Doukas et al. [2002], Teoh and Wong [2002], Bradshaw et al. [2006], and Piotroski and So [2012]). Consistent with this interpretation, So [2013] shows that investors overweight analyst forecasts of future earnings and underweight fundamental information that identifies predictable variation in analyst forecast errors. This evidence suggests that predictable variation in analyst forecast errors may signal that investors and analysts misprice the same underlying signals because they rely on analysts as information intermediaries.

Tests based on the direction of future analyst forecast revisions allow the researcher to directly measure expectation errors and belief revisions for a set of sophisticated market participants. Because they are not return-based, these tests overcome concerns that results are confounded by imperfect risk controls.

6.5 Sub-periods and sub-populations

Academic research on return predictability often begins by documenting an association between a given signal and future returns within a large pooled sample of firms across many years. While such evidence might be suggestive of a pricing anomaly, it is at best an in-sample fit; it does not represent an implementable (or "tradable" strategy).

More robust tests call for evidence of return predictability across sub-periods and over sub-populations of firms. Segmentation by time period is important for several reasons. The first is to document whether the pattern is stable over time. Stability indicates that the return pattern is reliably present, which adds confidence that the results are not driven by a statistical aberration confined to a given window of time. The second is that in order for a strategy to be implementable in real-time (that is, by tradable), portfolio construction must occur at specific points in time. To avoid peek-ahead bias, all the relevant information must already be available at the time of portfolio construction.

A common application of tests that examine the stability of return predictability over time is attributed to Fama and MacBeth [1973]. The so-called "Fama–MacBeth" tests estimate the relation between returns and a set of controls, which typically consists of a candidate signal and a set of proxies that control for the asset's risk exposure. The regressions are estimated across multiple time periods (for example, regressions are estimated monthly or annually) to determine whether a given firm characteristic displays a stable relation with returns across multiple time periods. The regression test is run each period and the significance of a relation between a firm characteristic and future returns is assessed across all periods in the sample.

The Fama–MacBeth approach is preferable to pooled regression tests because it offers evidence on the consistency of the strategy over time. An important caveat to this analysis is that a stable relation between a given signal and future returns does not in itself speak to the issue of risk versus mispricing. Indeed, some proponents of market efficiency argue that stable relations are more likely to reflect compensation for risk, because true mispricing should decline over time as additional capital is deployed to correct the biased expectations embedded in market prices.

Another good reason for researchers to partition their analyses over time is to identify how return predictability varies with macroeconomic conditions. If a given strategy's returns are attributable to risk, it should experience particularly bad performance during 'bad' states of the world, such as in recessions or over periods of extreme market decline, because these are periods in which investors' marginal utility for wealth is highest. An excellent example of this can be found in Lakonishok et al. [1994], who document returns to various contrarian (value/glamour) strategies over different economic conditions. They find that during recessions these strategies perform at least as well and sometimes better than relative to non-recessionary periods. These findings cast doubt on risk-based explanations that rely on time-varying discount rates to explain the value premium (see, for example, Zhang [2005]).

A third reason that researchers examine variation in return predictability across sub-periods is that it provides insights into whether

inefficiencies appear to decline over time as investors learn of existing mispricing. For example, Green et al. [2011] show that the accrual
anomaly originally documented in Sloan [1996] declines over time
in response to increases in the supply of arbitrage capital commit-
ted to trading on abnormal accruals. Similarly, in a recent working
paper, McLean and Pontiff [2013] survey 82 strategies identified in academic research that predict returns and shows that post-publication
predictability significantly declines whereas trading activity associated
with the strategies significantly increases. These findings are more pronounced in larger and more liquidity securities, suggesting that market frictions contribute the evidence of predictable returns. Similarly,
by exploiting time-variation in market frictions such as lending constraints on capital and behavioral biases such as investor irrationality,
researchers are able to examine whether time-varying returns reflect
differences in market frictions and/or market sentiment.

Researchers often also examine how return predictability varies
across sub-populations. One of the most common examples of this
practice is to examine how the signal–return relation varies across subsamples segmented by firm size. This practice reflects the fact that limits to arbitrage and information gathering costs are higher for smaller
firms than for larger firms. The use of subsamples can also offer insight
into the robustness of the strategy variations across industries, bid–ask
spreads, analyst coverage, information uncertainty, and other measures
of market liquidity.

6.6 Delisting and survivorship biases

When examining the profitability of a given strategy, it is important
that researchers account for data artifacts and empirical design choices
that can artificially inflate statistical evidence of the strategy's return.
One example of a data artifact that can inflate returns is delisting bias,
first raised by Shumway [1997]. Delisting bias occurs when researchers
fail to account for an asset's disappearance from a given dataset, which
commonly occurs when a firm becomes bankrupt or becomes delisted
from a stock exchange such as Nasdaq or NYSE. Shumway [1997] points

out that many firms delist due to bankruptcy and/or adverse firm performance but researchers may attribute the absence of the firm from a dataset as an indication that the asset earns a zero return, rather than the correct delisting return. For example, when a firm delists from one of the major U.S. stock exchanges, it typically continues to trade but at a significantly lower price on an over-the-counter (OTC) market. Shumway [1997] points out that the average devaluation that results from delisting is between -35% and -50%. Thus, researchers are likely to significantly overstate the returns to strategies that purchase firms that are more likely to delist when failing to account for the delisting return.

A related issue is survivorship bias, which occurs when researchers bias the sample selection process to firms that are present in available datasets after a given event or period of time (that is, that survived until the date that the data was collected), rather than the full sample of firms that would have been available to an investor at the time of the initial investment decision as described in the proposed strategy. In the presence of survivorship bias, the portion of the sample not included in the researcher's sample would be not be randomly selected and instead biased toward more extreme performance outcomes such as bankruptcy, closure, delisting, or merger. Survivorship bias commonly occurs when researchers or data providers start with a sample of firms that are present in a database as of a point in time and trace this set of firms back in history. Survivorship bias more commonly hides extreme poor performance from the researcher's dataset and can thus inflate reported performance metrics. Researchers should employ techniques to mitigate these biases when the end return is not available. For example, Shumway [1997] suggests determining the reason for a firm's delisting and then incorporating the average delisting return for firms that delist for similar reasons.

6.7   Size, illiquidity and exploitability issues

Evidence of predictable returns is distinct from evidence of mispricing when the returns do not reflect available economic profits in the spirit of Jensen [1978]. Though there are varying benchmarks for establishing mispricing, one common benchmark is that return predictability reflects evidence of available economic profits that are exploitable in the sense that they exceed the costs of implementing the underlying strategy. Under this interpretation, mispricing indicates that investors could implement a given strategy and receive positive risk-adjusted profits after accounting for transaction costs.

Several factors contribute to whether a given strategy is exploitable such as transaction costs and capital constraints [Malkiel and Fama, 1970]. Investors incur transaction costs when implementing trading strategies and these can and often have a material impact on whether the investors' net wealth increases or decreases as a result of trading. For example, when buying or selling shares of a security, investors commonly incur costs related to the security's bid–ask spreads. In modern markets, liquidity providers facilitate trades by matching buy and sell orders as well as absorbing order imbalances into their own account. Because market makers face adverse selection risks, inventory holding risks, and order processing costs related to trade settlement and reporting and order routing, market makers generally quote "ask" prices, reflecting the price at which they are willing to purchase securities, that exceed "bid" prices, reflecting the price at which they are willing to sell securities [Glosten and Harris, 1988, Huang and Stoll, 1997]. By purchasing shares at lower prices then the price at which they sell, market makers capture the bid–ask spread. From the investor's perspective, a positive bid–ask spread means that the realized transaction price will differ from closing prices used to calculate returns. For example, purchasing shares at the ask means that the investor will pay a price higher than the midpoint quote, which has the effect of reducing future returns. Thus, failing to account for differences between available transaction prices and average or closing prices can inflate the returns that an investor may experience when attempting to implement a given strategy.

More generally, the presence of transaction costs implies that observed patterns of returns do not equate to available economic profits. A common approach to test for evidence of mispricing is to examine whether a given signal predicts returns among larger firms, where transaction costs are less likely to be binding (see, for example, Fama and French [2008]). Although the absence of return predictability among larger firms could be due to factors distinct from liquidity, such as media attention or investor sentiment, researchers should be more skeptical when evidence on return predictability is highly concentrated among extremely small firms where transaction costs are likely to be economically large. When this concentration is evident in the data, it also raises concerns about the ability of investment professionals to exploit evidence of predictable returns because many investment outfits impose a minimum size or liquidity requirement before incorporating a position into its investment strategies.

A more rigorous but computationally intensive approach to look for evidence of available economic profits is to directly compute returns earned after accounting for transaction cost estimates (see, for example, Amihud and Mendelson [1980], Lesmond et al. [1999], and Hasbrouck [2009]). These studies provide direct estimates of the cost of entering or exiting a position to allow researchers and practitioners to assess whether a given strategy will yield profits after accounting for transaction costs. This approach has been used in studies on post-earnings announcement drift (PEAD) such as Sadka [2006] and Ng et al. [2008]. These studies conclude that much of the anomalous returns to PEAD strategies are attributable to large transaction costs around earnings announcements that prevent investors from making profitable trades that incorporate earnings information into market prices.

6.8   Gauging economic significance

Evidence of returns predictability is typically presented in academic studies in the form of hypothetical returns that an investor would earn by implementing the strategy. These estimated "paper profits" are commonly compounded and expressed as an annualized rate of return, often after some sort of risk adjustment. Although an annualized risk-adjusted return measure is important, taken alone, it does not offer a full picture of economic significance.

The economic significance of a pricing anomaly is ultimately rooted in how much alpha, in dollar terms, an investor could extract through careful implementation of a proposed signal. For example, strategies that generate high average annualized returns but that are applicable only to a small number of firms, or to infrequently occurring events, are unlikely to be as economically significant as more broadly applicable signals, such as momentum or value. These more narrowly-applicable signals are likely to generate a relatively small amount of dollar alpha. Similarly, strategies that generate high average annualized returns but are concentrated in small and illiquid stocks also are unlikely to generate high dollar alphas after extraction costs.

Thus, when evaluating evidence of return predictability, we encourage researchers to evaluate economic significance along three principle dimensions: (1) Annualized returns, (2) Breadth (also known as the 'applicability' of the strategy), and (3) Scale (also known as the 'capacity' for the strategy).

(1) **Annualized returns** simply refer to the hypothetical percentage return generated through implementing a proposed strategy, reinvesting the proceeds of liquidated positions, and compounding the returns over the course of a year. To create comparability across studies, these returns are typically, though certainly not necessarily, expressed gross of transaction cost estimates. These returns are hypothetical in the sense that they do not reflect gains from implementing the strategy with actual trades and are commonly referred to as "paper profits."

(2) **Breadth** refers to the number of investment opportunities (for example, firms or events) that occur within a given time period where the proposed signal is observable for trading. For example, strategies based purely on return momentum have high levels of breadth because constructing the underlying signal only requires conditioning upon lagged return data. As a result, momentum strategies can be applied to the vast majority of publicly traded companies, commonly encompassing thousands of firms each period (for example, calendar weeks or months). High levels of breadth are appealing because (1) they allow researchers

greater flexibility in layering or combining signals, such as trading on momentum and value simultaneously, (2) they allow for stricter sample selection criterion, such as greater size and liquidity requirements, and (3) they make it more likely that researchers and investors can form synchronized portfolios utilizing simultaneous long and short positions to hedge unintended risk exposures. By contrast, signals based on infrequent events, such as earnings announcements or managerial forecasts, offer lower levels of breadth because they are only applicable within the event period and thus are commonly non-synchronized.

(3) **Scale** refers to the ability of a proposed strategy to remain profitable when the dollar amount of capital being deployed increases. When investors face large execution costs and price impact, annualized returns overstate the extent to which strategies can generate alpha. As discussed in Section 5, studies by Frazzini et al. [2012] use live trading data to assess the capacity of value, size, momentum, and price-reversal strategies across various capital markets around the world. Although live trading data or even direct estimates of transaction costs for the marginal investor can be difficult to obtain, studies that examine the sensitivity of a strategy to equal- versus value-weighting shed light on a strategy's capacity because they indicate the extent to which return predictability holds among larger, more liquid firms that presumably face lower transaction costs. Researchers can similarly estimate or assess a strategy's capacity by examining returns across NYSE/AMEX/Nasdaq market capitalization breakpoints or among portfolios sorted by liquidity proxies, where the goal is to gauge a strategy's resilience to lower costs of implementation.

6.9 Testing statistical significance

In assessing evidence of predictable returns, researchers face two related questions: First, do the returns reflect risk, mispricing, or both? Second, what is the statistical strength of the predictable return pattern? Once an appropriate performance benchmark or asset-pricing test is identified, the latter question is important in assessing the null that excess returns are reliably different than zero. In doing so, significance tests speak to the tradeoff between a strategy's returns and its underling risks. Reflecting the importance of this tradeoff, researchers commonly quote t-statistics as a close analogue to Sharpe Ratios because both compare a strategy's average return relative to its standard deviation.

Significance testing within asset-pricing studies, much like risk-adjustments, is complicated by the need for appropriate underlying assumptions. Standard regression techniques, such as ordinary least squares (OLS), are built upon the assumption that the regression residuals are independently and identically distributed (IID). For example, regression-based tests of a candidate signal commonly take the following form:

$$R_{i,t} = \alpha + \beta_i, \text{SIGNAL} + \varepsilon, \qquad (6.3)$$

where $R_{i,t}$ is the realized return, SIGNAL is the candidate signal, and ε is the regression residual. However, a common problem with tests of the form in Equation (3) is that the residuals can be correlated across firms and/or time, which violates an underlying assumption in the use of OLS and introduces bias into the estimated standard errors used for statistical significance tests. For example, the Fama–MacBeth regression tests discussed above are built upon the assumption that the returns of a given firm are uncorrelated over time. When this assumption is violated, standard errors can be biased downward because the estimated coefficients from each time period are incorrectly treated as being independent, leading to researchers to over-reject the null of insignificant returns.

Using both simulated and realized data, Peterson [2010] provides an excellent overview of significance testing, the severity of bias introduced through improper estimates of standard errors, and simple techniques for conducting asset-pricing tests, which depend on the given research setting or application. Peterson [2010] concludes that clustering standard errors provide a simple and effective approach for a broad array of asset-pricing tests to correct for violations of the assumption that regression residuals are IID.

When the IID assumption fails, standard regression techniques may understate the standard errors by incorrectly treating observations as independent, either across time periods or across specific subsamples. Clustering can mitigate biases resulting from failures of the IID assumption by using the estimated covariance matrix of these residuals and adjusting standard error estimates to account for the lack of independence. Gow et al. [2010] reach a similar conclusion in the context of the accounting literature and show that failure to account for clustering can lead researchers to incorrectly reject the null hypothesis. Together, these studies demonstrate the importance of properly specifying the assumptions underlying significance tests and highlight the need for robustness checks to ensure that a researcher's significance test is properly specified.

6.10 Long-window returns

A substantial literature in finance and accounting examines predictable patterns in returns measured over long-windows, commonly ranging from one to five years. The use of long-window returns is potentially advantageous in mimicking the returns to a long-term investor and in identifying predictable patterns in returns that vary with the length of the return window, such as long-term return reversals. The use of long-window returns, however, is also potentially problematic because the researcher's inference can be highly sensitive to the chosen testing methodology. For example, in his survey of anomalies, Fama [1998] argues "most long-term return anomalies tend to disappear with reasonable changes in technique."[3]

Consistent with Fama's arguments, Kothari and Warner [1997] and Barber and Lyon [1997] show that researchers' inferences are

---

[3]Loughran and Ritter [2000], however, point out that value-weighted tests offer the least power for detecting mispricing because misvaluations are intuitively most pronounced among small firms and because value-weighting can cause most of the returns to be driven by a small handful of extremely large firms. They conclude that it is thus not only unsurprising, but actually expected, that anomaly returns dissipate among value-weighted return tests.

commonly sensitive to the research methodology. Kothari and Warner [1997] use simulation analyses to show that standard regression and significance tests involving long-horizon returns around firm-specific events are significantly misspecified. The misspecification can result from the assumption that long-horizon returns have a zero mean and unit standard deviation, which fail to hold due to several related phenomena such as pre-event survivorship bias and right-skewness in the distribution of long-window returns. To mitigate these issues, Kothari and Warner [1997] recommend nonparametric tests or bootstrap procedures, which allow significance tests to reflect the distribution of returns specific to the sample being considered.

In a related study, Barber and Lyon [1997] show that proper inferences from long-window abnormal return tests require that researchers select the proper benchmark to measure an abnormal or unexpected change in price. Using simulation tests, Barber and Lyon show that failing to identify the proper benchmark can lead to biased inferences because the resulting return distribution does not have a zero mean and unit standard deviation. For example, the use of index returns can introduce new-listing, rebalancing, and skewness biases in the distribution of long-horizon returns, which violate the distributional assumptions underlying standard significance tests. To mitigate these biases, Barber and Lyon [1997] make several recommendations including using characteristic-matched portfolios, using firms' size and book-to-market ratio, as the basis for judging abnormal returns. Daniel et al. [1997] extend these findings by showing that characteristic-matching improves when also selecting benchmarks based on firms' return momentum and by providing a simple technique for estimating characteristic-based reference portfolios.

In a recent survey, Ang and Zhang [2015] expand upon Kothari and Warner [1997] and Barber and Lyon [1997] by discussing in more depth a broad array of complications that can arise in long-horizon event studies as well as techniques for addressing them. Together, this literature underscores the need for caution when evaluating evidence of long-horizon abnormal returns.

6.11   Incremental contribution

Most of the preceding text in this section concerns the adjudication of risk versus mispricing as explanations for observed patterns in returns. However, researchers are often equally concerned about whether the documented evidence is likely to make an incremental contribution to the academic literature. These concerns are related because academic journals care not only about how the world looks but also why it looks a certain way.

In documenting predictability in returns, how should researchers gauge whether such evidence is likely to make an incremental academic contribution and thus worthwhile to pursue as part of an academic study? From our perspective, papers that provide an incremental contribution generally satisfy *at least* one of the following criteria:

(1) Signal Identification: the paper identifies and validates a new signal or data source that offers strong predictive power for returns. Importantly, the new signal or data source must be distinct from prior research. Even if such a paper does not establish why the mispricing exists it can provide a contribution by bringing the new evidence to light and encouraging future researchers to study the underlying mechanisms.

A classic example of signal identification is Jegadeesh and Titman [1993], who documented returns to strategies based on return momentum. In documenting momentum strategy returns, Jegadeesh and Titman [1993] do not identify why such patterns exist but provide the literature with a startling new finding — in terms of its economic magnitude, pervasiveness across subpopulations of stocks, consistency over time, and direct implications for the EMH. Due to these attributes, the evidence in Jegadeesh and Titman [1993] serves as "conversation starter" that provides a foundation for further research to understand the source of this widespread and economically large predictability in the cross-section of returns. It is relatively rare that studies satisfy the signal identification criteria as well as Jegadeesh and Titman

[1993], which helps to explain why the study has such a profound impact on research in finance, economics, and accounting.

(2) Mechanism Identification: the paper convincingly demonstrates an underlying mechanism (for example, market frictions or behavioral biases) that gives rise to predictability in returns. Satisfying this criterion requires clean identification to separate competing and related explanations. These types of studies can either identify a mechanism contemporaneously with documenting new evidence of return predictability or serve as a follow-up study that builds upon prior studies focused on signal identification.

Bernard and Thomas [1990] is a classic example of research that makes an incremental contribution by identifying an explanation for post-earnings announcement drift (PEAD). The Bernard and Thomas [1990] study is referenced repeatedly throughout this section precisely because it employs a battery of tests that adjudicate risk- versus mispricing-based explanations for PEAD and, in doing so, provides evidence that PEAD is driven by investors underreacting to positive time-series correlations in firms' earnings news.

(3) Methodological Refinement: the paper offers a significant refinement of previously established signals that afford researchers with greater power or precision to quantify and understand the underlying mechanisms. Methodological refinement papers differ from signal identification studies because they tend to refine existing ideas or signals, rather than introducing a new concept or class of signals.

A great example of a study offering methodological refinement is Richardson et al. [2005], which serves a follow-on study on the evidence of the accrual anomaly documented in Sloan [1996]. Richardson et al. [2005] refine the Sloan study by linking the reliability of accruals to earnings persistence. Specifically, the authors use firms' balance sheets to categorize each component of accruals and show that the less reliable components have lower earnings persistence. The authors show that the accrual anomaly is driven by the less reliable component of accruals and, thus, that research focused on the sources and implications of the accrual anomaly should incorporate variation in the reliability of accruals.

Satisfying at least one of the above criteria is a necessary, but not sufficient, condition for establishing an incremental contribution. By providing these guidelines, we hope to help researchers get a sense of whether a result is likely to make an incremental contribution and thus worthwhile to pursue as part of an academic study.

Summary

Evidence of return predictability provides a fertile ground of inquiry for understanding the forces and mechanisms that shape asset prices. The influence of risk-averse traders with limited cognitive processing opens the doors for both risk and mispricing to give rise to predictability in asset returns. A central goal of research in this area is to distinguish these non-mutually exclusive explanations.

In this section, we have outlined several techniques that researchers can use to distinguish risk from mispricing. We suggest that researchers first suppose that all return predictability is driven by risk, and then ask what would the risk look like and how would it have to operate in order to give rise the observed returns? Using this characterization helps guide the researcher in developing other testable hypotheses of what additional patterns we would expect to observe, or not observe, under a risk-based framework. In addition, we advocate the use of short-window returns around information events, sub-population analysis, and non-return-based measures of investors' expectations in identifying the source of predictable asset returns.

In addition to risk and mispricing, this section offers a brief survey of exploitability issues in studies involving predictable asset returns. Transaction costs may dissuade informed investors from impounding information into asset prices, which can give rise to predictability in asset returns, even in the absence of risk or mispricing. Evidence of predictable returns is distinct from evidence of mispricing when the returns do not reflect available economic profits in the spirit of Jensen [1978]. A central theme of this section is to provide researchers with methodological tools for distinguishing these channels and to promote the development of further tests useful in understanding the source of predictability in asset returns.

Acknowledgements

We are grateful to Nick Guest, David Hirshleifer, Ken Li, Charles McClure, Trung Nguyen, Kent Womack, Teri Yohn, and Christina Zhu for their helpful comments and suggestions. We also greatly appreciate the thoughtful input of Scott Richardson (Reviewer) and Stephen Penman (Editor). Finally, a special thanks to Stefan Reichelstein for not allowing us to give up on this project.

References

V. V. Acharya and L. Pedersen. Asset pricing with liquidity risk. *Journal of Financial Economics*, 77:375–410, 2005.

T. Adrian, E. Etula, and T. Muir. Financial intermediaries and the cross-section of asset returns. *Journal of Finance*, 69:2557–2596, 2014.

J. Affleck-Graves and R. Miller. The information content of calls of debt: Evidence from long-run stock returns. *Journal of Financial Research*, 26: 421–447, 2003.

A. Ahmed, E. Kilic, and G. Lobo. Does recognition versus disclosure matter? evidence from value-relevance of banks' recognized and disclosed derivative financial instruments. *The Accounting Review*, 81:567–588, 2006.

F. Akbas, W. J. Armstrong, S. Sorescu, and A. Subrahmanyam. Smart money, dumb money, and capital market anomalies. *Journal of Financial Economics*, 118:355–382, 2015.

E. Altman. Financial ratios, discriminant analysis, and the prediction of corporate bankruptcy. *Journal of Finance*, 23:589–609, 1968.

Y. Amihud and H. Mendelson. Asset pricing and the bid-ask spread. *Journal of Financial Economics*, 17:223–249, 1986.

S. Anderson and J. Born. Closed-end fund pricing: Theory and evidence. In *The Innovations in Financial Markets and Institutions series*, Springer, 2002.

A. Ang, R. Hodrick, Y. Xing, and X. Zhang. The cross-section of volatility and expected returns. *Journal of Finance*, 61:259–299, 2006.

J. Ang and S. Zhang. Evaluating long-horizon event study methodology. In *Handbook of Financial Econometrics and Statistics*, Springer, New York, 2015.

S. Arif and C. Lee. Aggregate investment and investor sentiment. *Review of Financial Studies*, 2015. Forthcoming.

S. Arif, A. Ben-Rephael, and C. Lee. Do short-sellers profit from mutual funds? evidence from daily trades. Working paper, University of Indiana and Stanford University, 2015.

H. Arkes, L. Herren, and A. Isen. The role of potential loss in the influence of affect on risk-taking behavior. *Organizational Behavior and Human Decision Processes*, 42:181–193, 1988.

C. Asness and J. Liew. The great divide over market efficiency. *Institutional Investor*, 2014. URL http://www.institutionalinvestor.com/Article/3315202/Asset-Management-Equities/The-Great-Divide-over-Market-Efficiency.html#.U6m8gfldXAk.

C. Asness, A. Frazzini, and L. Pedersen. Quality minus junk. Working paper, AQR Capital Management and New York University, 2013.

C. Asness, A. Frazzini, R. Israel, and T. Moskowitz. Fact, fiction, and momentum investing. *Journal of Portfolio Management*, 40:75–92, 2014.

P. Asquith, P. A. Pathak, and J. R. Ritter. Short interest, institutional ownership, and stock returns. *Journal of Financial Economics*, 78:243–276, 2005.

M. Bagnoli, M. B. Clement, and S. G. Watts. Around-the-clock media coverage and the timing of earnings announcements. Working Paper, Purdue University, 2005.

M. Baker and J. Wurgler. The equity share in new issues and aggregate stock returns. *Journal of Finance*, 55:2219–2257, 2000.

M. Baker and J. Wurgler. Market timing and capital structure. *Journal of Finance*, 57:1–32, 2002.

M. Baker and J. Wurgler. Investor sentiment and the cross-section of stock returns. *Journal of Finance*, 61:1645–1680, 2006.

M. Baker and J. Wurgler. Investor sentiment in the stock market. *Journal of Economic Perspectives*, 21:129–151, 2007.

M. Baker and J. Wurgler. Behavioral corporate finance: An updated survey. In *Handbook of the Economics of Finance*, Volume 2. Elsevier Press, 2012.

M. Baker, J. Wurgler, and Y. Yuan. Global, local, and contagious investor sentiment. *Journal of Financial Economics*, 104:272–287, 2012.

T. G. Bali, N. Calcici, and R. F. Whitelaw. Maxing out: Stocks as lotteries and the cross-section of expected returns. *Journal of Financial Economics*, 99:427–446, 2011.

B. Barber and J. Lyon. Detecting long-run abnormal stock returns: The empirical power and specification of test statistics. *Journal of Financial Economics*, 43:341–372, 1997.

B. Barber and T. Odean. All that glitters: The effect of attention and news on the buying behavior of individual and institutional investors. *Review of Financial Studies*, 21:785–818, 2008.

B. Barber and T. Odean. The behavior of individual investors. In *Handbook of the Economics of Finance,* Volume 2. Elsevier Press, 2015.

B. Barber, Y. Lee, Y. Liu, and T. Odean. Just how much do individual investors lose by trading? *Review of Financial Studies*, 22:609–632, 2009a.

B. Barber, T. Odean, and N. Zhu. Do retail trades move markets? *Review of Financial Studies*, 22:151–186, 2009b.

N. Barberis. Thirty years of prospect theory in economics: A review and assessment. *Journal of Economic Perspectives*, 27:173–196, 2013.

N. Barberis and M. Huang. Stocks as lotteries: The implications of probability weighting for security prices. *American Economic Review*, 98:2066–2100, 2008.

N. Barberis and A. Shleifer. Style investing. *Journal of Financial Economics*, 68:161–199, 2003.

N. Barberis and R. Thaler. A survey of behavioral finance. In *Handbook of the Economics of Finance*. Elsevier Press, 2002.

N. Barberis, A. Shleifer, and R. Vishny. A model of investor sentiment. *Journal of Financial Economics*, 49:307–343, 1998.

N. Barberis, M. Huang, and T. Santos. Prospect theory and asset prices. *Quarterly Journal of Economics*, 116:1–53, 2001.

N. Barberis, A. Shleifer, and J. Wurgler. Comovement. *Journal of Financial Economics*, 75:283–317, 2004.

N. Barberis, R. Greenwood, L. Jin, and A. Shleifer. X-capm: An extrapolative capital asset pricing model. *Journal of Financial Economics*, 115:1–24, 2015.

M. Barth, W. Beaver, and W. Landsman. The relevance of the value relevance literature for financial accounting standard setting: Another view. *Journal of Accounting and Economics*, 31:77–104, 2001.

S. Basu. The investment performance of common stocks in relation to their price-to-earnings: A test of the efficient markets hypothesis. *Journal of Finance*, 32:663–682, 1977.

R. Battalio and P. Schultz. Regulatory uncertainty and market liquidity: The 2008 short sale ban's impact on equity option markets. *Journal of Finance*, 66:2013–2053, 2011.

L. A. Bebchuk, A. Cohen, and C. C. Y. Wang. Learning and the disappearing association between governance and returns. *Journal of Financial Economics*, 108:323–348, 2013.

A. Ben-Rephael, S. Kandel, and A. Wohl. Measuring investor sentiment with mutual fund flows. *Journal of Financial Economics*, 104:363–382, 2012.

M. Beneish. The detection of earnings manipulation. *Financial Analysts Journal*, 55:24–36, 1999.

M. Beneish, C. Lee, and C. Nichols. Earnings manipulation and expected returns. *Financial Analysts Journal*, 69:57–82, 2013.

M. Beneish, C. Lee, and C. Nichols. In short supply: Short-sellers and stock returns. *Journal of Accounting and Economics*, 2015. Forthcoming.

J. Berk and R. C. Green. Mutual fund flows and performance in rational markets. *Journal of Political Economy*, 112:1269–1295, 2004.

J. Berk and J. van Binsbergen. Measuring skill in the mutual fund industry. *Journal of Financial Economics*, 2014. Forthcoming.

V. Bernard. The Feltham-Ohlson framework: Implications for empiricists. *Contemporary Accounting Research*, 11:733–747, 1995.

V. Bernard and K. Schipper. Recognition and disclosure in financial reporting. Working paper, University of Michigan and University of Chicago, 1994.

V. Bernard and J. K. Thomas. Evidence that stock prices do not fully reflect the implications of current earnings for future earnings. *Journal of Accounting and Economics*, 13:305–341, 1990.

S. Bhojraj and C. Lee. Who is my peer? A valuation-based approach to the selection of comparable firms. *Journal of Accounting Research*, 40:407–439, 2002.

M. Billett, M. Flannery, and J. Garfinkel. Are bank loans special? Evidence on the post-announcement performance of bank borrowers. *Journal of Financial and Quantitative Analysis*, 41:733–751, 2006.

F. Black. Presidential address: Noise. *Journal of Finance*, 41:529–543, 1986.

F. Black, M. Jensen, and M. Scholes. The capital asset pricing model: Some empirical tests. In *Studies in the Theory of Capital Markets*, pages 79–121, Praeger, New York, 1972.

E. Blankespoor. The impact of information processing costs on firm disclosure choice: Evidence from the XBRL mandate. Working paper, Stanford University, 2013.

J. Blocher, A. Reed, and E. Van Wesep. Connecting two markets: An equilibrium framework for shorts, longs, and stock loans. *Journal of Financial Economics*, 108:302–322, 2013.

J. Bodurtha, D. Kim, and C. Lee. Closed-end country funds and u.s. market sentiment. *Review of Financial Studies*, 8:879–918, 1995.

E. Boehmer and J. J. Wu. Short selling and the price discovery process. *Review of Financial Studies*, 26:287–322, 2013.

E. Boehmer, C. M. Jones, and X. Zhang. Shackling the short sellers: The 2008 shorting ban. Working paper, Singapore Management University, Columbia Business School, and Purdue University, 2012.

B. Boyer. Style-related comovements: Fundamentals or labels? *Journal of Finance*, 66:307–322, 2011.

M. Bradshaw, S. Richardson, and R. Sloan. The relation between corporate financing activities, analysts' forecasts and stock returns. *Journal of Accounting and Economics*, 42:53–85, 2006.

A. Brav and P. A. Gompers. Myth or reality? The long-run underperformance of initial public offerings: Evidence from venture capital and nonventure capital-backed companies. *Journal of Finance*, 52:1791–1822, 1997.

A. Bris, W. N. Goetzmann, and N. Zhu. Efficiency and the bear: Short sales and markets around the world. *Journal of Finance*, 62:1029–1079, 2007.

N. Brown, K. Wei, and R. Wermers. Analyst recommendations, mutual fund herding, and overreaction in stock prices. *Management Science*, 60:1–20, 2013.

M. K. Brunnermeier and S. Nagel. Hedge funds and the technology bubble. *Journal of Finance*, 59:2013–2040, 2004.

M. K. Brunnermeier and A. Parker. Optimal expectations. *American Economic Review*, 95:1092–1118, 2005.

M. K. Brunnermeier and L. Pedersen. Market liquidity and funding liquidity. *Review of Financial Studies*, 22:2201–2238, 2009.

M. K. Brunnermeier, C. Gollier, and A. Parker. Optimal beliefs, asset prices, and the preference for skewed returns. *American Economic Review*, 97: 159–165, 2007.

A. C. Call, M. Hewitt, T. Shevlin, and T. L. Yohn. Firm-specific estimates of differential persistence and their incremental usefulness for forecasting and valuation. *The Accounting Review*, 2015. forthcoming.

J. Campbell. A variance decomposition for stock returns. *Economic Journal*, 101:157–179, 1991.

J. Campbell. Empirical asset pricing: Eugene Fama, Lars Peter Hansen, and Robert Shiller. Working Paper, Harvard University and NBER, 2014.

J. Campbell and A. Kyle. Smart money, noise trading, and stock price behavior. *Review of Economic Studies*, 60:1–34, 1993.

J. Campbell and R. Shiller. Cointegration and tests of present value models. *Journal of Political Economy*, 95:1062–1087, 1987.

J. Campbell and R. Shiller. The dividend-price ratio and expectations of future dividends and discount factors. *Review of Financial Studies*, 1:195–228, 1988a.

J. Campbell and R. Shiller. Stock prices, earnings, and expected dividends. *Journal of Finance*, 43:661–676, 1988b.

J. Campbell, J. Hilscher, and J. Szilagyi. In search of distress risk. *Journal of Finance*, 63:2899–2939, 2008.

J. Campbell, C. Polk, and T. Vuolteenaho. Growth or glamour? Fundamentals and systematic risk in stock returns. *Review of Financial Studies*, 23:306–344, 2010.

M. Cao and J. Wei. Stock market returns: A note on temperature anomaly. *Journal of Banking and Finance*, 29:1559–1573, 2005.

M. Carhart. On persistence in mutual fund performance. *Journal of Finance*, 52:57–82, 1997.

M. Carlson, A. Fisher, and R. Giammarino. Corporate investment and asset price dynamics: Implications for seo event studies and long-run performance. *Journal of Finance*, 61:1009–1034, 2006.

J. Cassidy. Annals of money: The price prophet. *The New Yorker*, February 7 2000.

G. Cespa and T. Foucault. Illiquidity contagion and liquidity crashes. *Review of Financial Studies*, 27:1615–1660, 2014.

K. Chan, P. H. Hendershott, and A. B. Sanders. Risk and return on real estate: Evidence from equity reits. *AREUEA Journal*, 18:431–452, 1990.

L. Chan, N. Jegadeesh, and J. Lakonishok. Momentum strategies. *Journal of Finance*, 51:1681–1713, 1996.

S. Chava and A. Purnanadam. Is default risk negatively related to stock returns? *Review of Financial Studies*, 2009. Forthcoming.

L. Chen, Z. Da, and X. Zhao. What drives stock price movements? *Review of Financial Studies*, 26:841–876, 2013.

N. Chen, R. Roll, and S. Ross. Economic forces and the stock market. *Journal of Business*, 59:383–403, 1986.

N. Chen, R. Kan, and M. Miller. Are discounts on closed-end funds a sentiment index? *Journal of Finance*, 48:795–800, 1993a.

N. Chen, R. Kan, and M. Miller. A rejoinder. *Journal of Finance*, 48:809–810, 1993b.

P. Chen and G. Zhang. How do accounting variables explain stock price movements? Theory and evidence. *Journal of Accounting and Economics*, 43:219–244, 2007.

M. Cherkes. Closed-end funds: A survey. *Annual Review of Financial Economics*, 4:431–445, 2012.

J. Chevalier and G. Ellison. Risk taking by mutual funds as a response to incentives. *Journal of Political Economy*, 105:1167–1200, 1997.

N. Chopra, C. Lee, A. Shleifer, and R. Thaler. Yes, closed-end fund discounts are a sentiment index. *Journal of Finance*, 48:801–808, 1993a.

N. Chopra, C. Lee, A. Shleifer, and R. Thaler. Summing up. *Journal of Finance*, 48:811–812, 1993b.

S. Christoffersen, D. Musto, and R. Wermers. Investor flows to asset managers: Causes and consequences. *Annual Review of Financial Economics*, 6:289–310, 2014.

J. Claus and J. Thomas. Equity premia as low as three percent? Empirical evidence from analysts' earnings forecasts for domestic and international stock markets. Working paper, Columbia University, 2000.

J. H. Cochrane. Production-based asset pricing and the link between stock returns and economic fluctuations. *Journal of Finance*, 46:209–37, 1991.

J. H. Cochrane. Presidential address: Discount rates. *Journal of Finance*, 66:1047–1108, 2011.

L. Cohen and A. Frazzini. Economic links and limited attention. *Journal of Finance*, 63:1977–2011, 2008.

L. Cohen and D. Lou. Complicated firms. *Journal of Financial Economics*, 91:383–400, 2012.

L. Cohen, C. Malloy, and L. Pomorski. Decoding inside information. *Journal of Financial Economics*, 91:1009–1043, 2012.

L. Cohen, K. Diether, and C. Malloy. Misvaluing innovation. *Review of Financial Studies*, 2013a. Forthcoming.

L. Cohen, K. Diether, and C. Malloy. Legislating stock prices. *Journal of Financial Economics*, 2013b. Forthcoming.

R. B. Cohen, C. Polk, and T. Vuolteenahu. The price is (almost) right. *Journal of Finance*, 64:2739–2782, 2009.

T. Copeland, A. Dolgoff, and A. Moel. The role of expectations in explaining the cross-section of stock returns. *Review of Accounting Studies*, 9:149–188, 2004.

S. Cottle, R. Murray, and F. Block. *Graham and Dodd's Security Analysis, Fifth Edition*. McGraw-Hill Book Company, 1988.

J. Coval and E. Stafford. Asset fire sales (and purchases) in equity markets. *Journal of Financial Economics*, 86:479–512, 2007.

J. D. Coval, D. A. Hirshleifer, and T. Shumway. Can individual investors beat the market? Working paper, Harvard University, 2005.

D. Cutler, J. Poterba, and L. Summers. What moves stock prices? *Journal of Portfolio Management*, 15:4–12, 1989.

Z. Da and M. Warachka. Cashflow risk, systematic earnings revisions, and the cross-section of stock returns. *Journal of Financial Economics*, 94:448–468, 2009.

Z. Da, J. Engelberg, and P. Gao. In search of attention. *Journal of Finance*, 66:1461–1499, 2011.

Z. Da, U. G. Gurun, and M. Warachka. Frog in the pan: Continuous information and momentum. *Review of Financial Studies*, 27:2171–2218, 2015.

A. Damodaran. Value investing: Investing for grown ups? Working paper, NYU, 2012.

K. Daniel and S. Titman. Evidence on the characteristics of cross-sectional variation in common stock returns. *Journal of Finance*, 52:1–33, 1997.

K. Daniel and S. Titman. Market reactions to tangible and intangible information. *Journal of Finance*, 61:1605–1643, 2006.

K. Daniel, M. Grinblatt, S. Titman, and R. Wermers. Measuring mutual fund performance with characteristic-based benchmarks. *Journal of Finance*, 52: 1035–1058, 1997.

K. Daniel, D. Hirshleifer, and A. Subrahmanyam. Investor psychology and security market under- and overreactions. *Journal of Finance*, 53:1839–1886, 1998.

K. Daniel, D. Hirshleifer, and A. Subrahmanyam. Overconfidence, arbitrage, and equilibrium asset pricing. *Journal of Finance*, 56:921–965, 2001.

H. Daouk, C. M. C. Lee, and D. Ng. Capital market governance: How do security laws affect market performance? *Journal of Corporate Finance*, 12:560–593, 2006.

G. D'Avolio. The market for borrowing stocks. *Journal of Financial Economics*, 66:271–306, 2002.

DBEQS Global, 2014. Academic Insights Month Report, Deutsche Bank Equity Quantitative Strategy Global.

W. DeBondt and R. Thaler. Does the stock market overreact? *Journal of Finance*, 40:793–805, 1985.

W. DeBondt and R. Thaler. Further evidence of investor overreaction and stock market seasonality. *Journal of Finance*, 42:557–581, 1987.

P. Dechow and R. Sloan. Returns to contrarian investment strategies: Tests of naive expectations hypotheses. *Journal of Financial Economics*, 43:3–27, 1997.

P. Dechow, A. Hutton, and R. Sloan. An empirical assessment of the residual income valuation model. *Journal of Accounting and Economics*, 26:1–34, 1999.

P. Dechow, A. Hutton, L. Meulbroek, and R. Sloan. Short-sellers, fundamental analysis, and stock returns. *Journal of Financial Economics*, 61:77–106, 2001.

P. Dechow, R. Sloan, and M. Soliman. Implied equity duration: A new measure of equity security risk. *Review of Accounting Studies*, 9:197–228, 2004.

D. Del Guercio. The distorting effect of the prudent-man laws on institutional equity investments. *Journal of Financial Economics*, 40:31–62, 1996.

S. Della Vigna and J. Pollet. Demographics and industry returns. *American Economic Review*, 97:1667–1702, 2007.

S. Della Vigna and J. Pollet. Investor inattention and Friday earnings announcements. *Journal of Finance*, 64:709–749, 2009.

J. DeLong, A. Shleifer, L. H. Summers, and R. J. Waldmann. Noise trader risk in financial markets. *Journal of Political Economy*, 98:703–738, 1990a.

J. DeLong, A. Shleifer, L. H. Summers, and R. J. Waldmann. Positive feedback investment strategies and destabilizing rational speculation. *Journal of Finance*, 45:379–395, 1990b.

E. Demers and C. Vega. Linguistic tone in earnings press releases: News or noise? Working paper, INSEAD and the Board of Governors of the Federal Reserve System, 2011.

D. K. Denis, J. J. McConnell, A. V. Ovtchinnikov, and Y. Yu. S&p 500 index additions and earnings expectations. *Journal of Finance*, 58:1821–1840, 2003.

H. Desai, K. Ramesh, S. R. Thiagarajan, and B. V. Balachandran. An investigation of the informational role of short interest in the nasdaq market. *The Journal of Finance*, 57:2263–2287, 2002.

H. Desai, S. Rajgopal, and M. Venkatachalam. Value-glamour and accrual-based market anomalies: One anomaly or two? *The Accounting Review*, 79: 355–385, 2004.

D. Diamond and R. E. Verrecchia. Information aggregation in a noisy rational expectations economy. *Journal of Financial Economics*, 9:221–236, 1981.

I. Dichev. Is the risk of bankruptcy a systematic risk? *Journal of Finance*, 53:1131–1147, 1998.

I. Dichev. What are stock investors' actual historical returns? Evidence from dollar-weighted returns. *American Economic Review*, 97:386–401, 2007.

I. Dichev and G. Yu. Higher risk, lower returns: What hedge fund investors really earn. *Journal of Financial Economics*, 100:248–263, 2011.

K. Diether, C. Malloy, and A. Scherbina. Differences of opinion and the cross-section of stock returns. *Journal of Finance*, 57:2113–2141, 2002.

M. Dong, D. Hirshleifer, and S. H. Teoh. Overvalued equity and financing decisions. *Review of Financial Studies*, 25:3645–3683, 2012.

J. Doukas, C. Kim, and C. Pantzalis. A test of the errors-in-expectations explanation of the value/glamour stock returns performance: Evidence from analysts' forecasts. *Journal of Finance*, 57:2143–2165, 2002.

M. Drake, L. Rees, and E. Swanson. Should investors follow the prophets or the bears? Evidence on the use of public information by analysts and short sellers. *The Accounting Review*, 86:101–130, 2011.

M. Drake, K. Gee, and J. Thornock. March market madness: The impact of value-irrelevant events on the market pricing of earnings news. *Contemporary Accounting Research*, 2015. Forthcoming.

T. Dyckman and D. Morse. *Efficient Capital Markets: A Critical Analysis.* Prentice-Hall, Englewood Cliffs, N.J, 2nd edition, 1986.

D. Easley and M. O'Hara. Information and the cost of capital. *Journal of Finance*, 59:1553–1583, 2004.

P. Easton. PE ratios, PEG ratios, and estimating the implied expected rate of return on equity capital. *The Accounting Review*, 79:73–96, 2004.

P. Easton and T. Harris. Earnings as an explanatory variable for returns. *Journal of Accounting Research*, 29:19–36, 1991.

P. Easton, T. Harris, and J. Ohlson. Aggregate accounting earnings can explain most of security returns. *Journal of Accounting and Economics*, 15:119–142, 1992.

A. Edmans, D. Garcia, and O. Norli. Sports sentiment and stock returns. *Journal of Finance*, 62:1967–1998, 2007.

E. Edwards and P. Bell. *The Theory and Measurement of Business Income.* University of California Press, Berkeley, CA, 1961.

D. Ellsberg. Risk, ambiguity, and the savage axioms. *Quarterly Journal of Economics*, 75:643–699, 1961.

E. Elton. Presidential address: Expected return, realized return, and asset pricing tests. *Journal of Finance*, 54:1199–1220, 1999.

C. Engel. Some new variance bounds for asset prices. *Journal of Money, Credit, and Banking*, 37:949–955, 2005.

J. Engelberg. Costly information processing: Evidence from earnings announcements. Working paper, Northwestern University, 2008.

J. Engelberg, A. V. Reed, and M. C. Ringgenberg. How are shorts informed? Short sellers, news, and information processing. *Journal of Financial Economics*, 105:260–278, 2012a.

J. Engelberg, C. Sasseville, and J. Williams. Market madness? The case of mad money. *Management Science*, 58:351–364, 2012b.

R. Engle, R. Ferstenberg, and J. Russell. Measuring and modeling execution cost and risk. *Journal of Portfolio Management*, 38:14–28, 2012.

E. Eyster, M. Rabin, and D. Vayanos. Financial markets where traders neglect the information content of prices. Working paper, London School of Economics and UC Berkeley, 2013.

F. J. Fabozzi, editor. *Short selling: Strategies, risks, and rewards.* Wiley and Sons, Hoboken, NJ, 2004.

E. Falkenstein. The missing risk premium: Why low volatility investing works. Working paper, Eric G. Falkenstein, 2012.

E. Fama. The behavior of stock market prices. *Journal of Business*, 38:34–105, 1965.

E. Fama. Efficient capital markets: A review of theory and empirical work. *Journal of Finance*, 25:1575–1617, 1970.

E. Fama. Efficient capital markets: II. *Journal of Finance*, 46:1575–1617, 1991.

E. Fama. Market efficiency, long-term returns, and behavioral finance. *Journal of Financial Economics*, 49:283–306, 1998.

E. Fama and K. French. The cross-section of expected stock returns. *Journal of Finance*, 47:427–465, 1992.

E. Fama and K. French. Common risk factors in the returns on stocks and bonds. *Journal of Financial Economics*, 33:3–56, 1993.

E. Fama and K. French. Industry costs of equity. *Journal of Finance*, 43: 153–193, 1997.

E. Fama and K. French. The equity premium. *Journal of Finance*, 57:637–659, 2002.

E. Fama and K. French. Dissecting anomalies. *Journal of Finance*, 63:1653–1678, 2008.

E. Fama and J. MacBeth. Risk, return, and equilibrium: Empirical tests. *Journal of Political Economy*, 81:607–636, 1973.

G. Feltham and J. Ohlson. Valuation and clean surplus accounting for operating and financial activities. *Contemporary Accounting Research*, 11:689–731, 1995.

G. Feltham and J. Ohlson. Residual earnings valuation with risk and stochastic interest rates. *The Accounting Review*, 74:165–183, 1999.

J. Francis, D. Pagach, and J. Stephan. The stock market response to earnings announcements released during trading versus nontrading periods. *Journal of Accounting Research*, 30:165–184, 1992.

J. Frankel and R. Meese. Are exchange rates excessively variable? In S. Fischer, editor, *NBER Macroeconomics Annual 1987*, pages 117–152, Cambridge, 1987. MIT Press.

R. Frankel and C. Lee. Accounting valuation, market expectation, and cross-sectional stock returns. *Journal of Accounting and Economics*, 25:283–319, 1998.

A. Frazzini and O. Lamont. Dumb money: Mutual fund flows and the cross-section of stock returns. *Journal of Financial Economics*, 88:299–322, 2008.

A. Frazzini and L. Pedersen. Betting against beta. *Journal of Financial Economics*, 111:1–15, 2014.

A. Frazzini, R. Israel, and T. J. Moskowitz. Trading cost of asset pricing anomalies. Working paper, AQR Capital Asset Management and University of Chicago, 2012.

K. French and R. Roll. Stock return variances: The arrival of information and the reaction of traders. *Journal of Financial Economics*, 17:5–26, 1986.

M. Friedman. The case for flexible exchange rates. In *Essays in Positive Economics*, Chicago, IL, 1953. University of Chicago Press.

K. Froot and E. Dabora. How are stock prices affected by location of trade? *Journal of Financial Economics*, 53:189–216, 1999.

W. Fung, D. A. Hsieh, N. Y. Naik, and T. Ramadorai. Hedge funds: Performance, risk, and capital formation. *Journal of Finance*, 63:1777–1803, 2008.

W. Gebhardt, C. Lee, and B. Swaminathan. Toward an implied cost of capital. *Journal of Accounting Research*, 39:135–176, 2001.

C. C. Geczy, D. K. Musto, and A. V. Reed. Stocks are special too: An analysis of the equity lending market. *Journal of Financial Economics*, 66:241–269, 2002.

T. George and C. Hwang. A resolution of the distress risk and leverage puzzles in the cross section of stock returns. *Journal of Financial Economics*, 96: 56–79, 2010.

S. Giglio and K. Shue. No news is news: Do markets underreact to nothing? *Review of Financial Studies*, 27:3389–3440, 2014.

C. Gleason and C. Lee. Analyst forecast revisions and market price discovery. *The Accounting Review*, 78:193–225, 2003.

L. Glosten and L. Harris. Estimating the components of the bid/ask spread. *Journal of Financial Economics*, 21:123–142, 1988.

W. N. Goetzmann and K. G. Rouwenhorst. Pairs trading: Performance of a relative-value arbitrage rule. *Review of Financial Studies*, 19:797–827, 2006.

I. Gow, G. Ormazabal, and D. Taylor. Correcting for cross-sectional and time-series dependence in accounting research. *The Accounting Review*, 85: 483–512, 2010.

B. Graham and D. Dodd. *Security Analysis: Principles and Techniques,* 1st Edition. McGraw-Hill, New York and London, 1934.

W. Gray and T. Carlisle. *Quantitative Value: A Practitioner's Guide to Automating Intelligent Investment and Eliminating Behavioral Errors.* Wiley and Sons, Hoboken, NJ, 2013.

J. Green, J. Hand, and M. Soliman. Going, going, gone? The apparent demise of the accruals anomaly. *Management Science*, 57:797–816, 2011.

J. Greenblatt. *The Little Book that Still Beats the Market.* Wiley and Sons, Hoboken, NJ, 2010.

D. Griffin and A. Tversky. The weighing of evidence and the determinants of confidence. *Cognitive Psychology*, 24:411–35, 1992.

R. Grinold and R. Kahn. *Active Portfolio Management: A Quantitative Approach for Producing Superior Returns and Controlling Risk,* 2nd Edition. McGraw-Hill, 1999.

S. Grossman and M. Miller. Liquidity and market structure. *Journal of Finance*, 43:617–643, 1988.

S. Grossman and J. Stiglitz. On the impossibility of informationally efficient markets. *American Economic Review*, 70:393–408, 1980.

K. Hanley, C. Lee, and P. Seguin. The marketing of closed-end fund ipos: Evidence from transactions data. *Journal of Financial Intermediation*, 5: 127–159, 1996.

S. G. Hanson and A. Sunderam. The growth and limits of arbitrage: Evidence from short interest. *Review of Financial Studies*, 27:1238–1286, 2014.

O. Hart and D. Kreps. Price destabilizing speculation. *Journal of Political Economy*, 94:927–952, 1986.

J. Hasbrouck. Trading costs and returns for us equities: Estimating effective costs from daily data. *Journal of Finance*, 64:1445–1477, 2009.

F. Hayek. *The Road to Serfdom.* George Routledge and Sons, London, UK, 1944.

F. Hayek. The use of knowledge in society. *American Economic Review*, 35: 519–530, 1945.

Z. He and A. Krishnamurthy. Intermediary asset pricing. *American Economic Review*, 103:732–770, 2013.

P. Healy and K. Palepu. Business analysis and valuation using financial statements, 5th edition. Cengage Learning, 2012.

Hines UK. The City UK Financial Markets Series Report on Fund Management, 2012.

D. Hirshleifer. Investor psychology and asset pricing. *Journal of Finance*, 56: 1533–1597, 2001.

D. Hirshleifer. A recent survey of behavioral finance. *Annual Review of Financial Economics*, 7, 2015.

D. Hirshleifer and T. Shumway. Good day sunshine: Stock returns and the weather. *Journal of Finance*, 58:1009–1032, 2003.

D. Hirshleifer and S. Teoh. Limited attention, information disclosure, and financial reporting. *Journal of Accounting and Economics*, 36:337–386, 2003.

D. Hirshleifer, S. Lim, and S. Teoh. Driven to distraction: Extraneous events and underreaction to earnings news. *Journal of Finance*, 64:2289–2325, 2009.

D. Hirshleifer, S. Lim, and S. Teoh. Limited investor attention and stock market misreactions to accounting information. *Review of Asset Pricing Studies*, 1:35–73, 2011a.

D. Hirshleifer, S. Teoh, and J. Yu. Short arbitrage, return asymmetry, and the accrual anomaly. *Review of Financial Studies*, 24:2429–2461, 2011b.

D. Hirshleifer, K. Hou, and S. Teoh. The accrual anomaly: Risk or mispricing? *Management Science*, 58:320–35, 2012.

E. Hirt, G. Erickson, C. Kennedy, and D. Zillmann. Costs and benefits of allegiance: Changes in fans' self-ascribed competencies after team victory versus defeat. *Journal of Personality and Social Psychology*, 63:724–738, 1992.

C. Ho and C. H. Hung. Investor sentiment as conditioning information in asset pricing. *Journal of Banking and Finance*, 33:892–903, 2009.

R. Holthausen and R. L. Watts. The relevance of the value-relevance literature for financial accounting standard setting. *Journal of Accounting and Economics*, 31:3–75, 2001.

H. Hong and J. Stein. A unified theory of underreaction, momentum trading and overreaction in asset markets. *Journal of Finance*, 54:2143–2184, 1999.

H. Hong, J. Kubik, and J. Stein. Social interaction and stock-market participation. *Journal of Finance*, 59:137–163, 2004.

K. Hou. Industry information diffusion and the lead-lag effect in stock returns. *Review of Financial Studies*, 20:1113–1138, 2007.

G. Hu, J. Pan, and J. Wang. Noise as information for illiquidity. *The Journal of Finance*, 68:2341–2382, 2013.

D. Huang, F. Jiang, J. Tu, and G. Zhou. Investor sentiment aligned: A powerful predictor of stock returns. *Review of Financial Studies*, 28:791–837, 2015.

R. Huang and H. Stoll. The components of the bid-ask spread: A general approach. *Review of Financial Studies*, 10:995–1034, 1997.

D. Ikenberry and S. Ramnath. Underreaction to self-selected news events: The case of stock splits. *Review of Financial Studies*, 15:489–526, 2002.

D. Ikenberry, J. Lakonishok, and T. Vermaelen. Market underreaction to open market share repurchases. *Journal of Financial Economics*, 39:181–208, 1995.

Z. Ivkovic and S. Weisbenner. Local does as local is: Information content of the geography of individual investors' common stock. *Journal of Finance*, 60:267–306, 2005.

Z. Ivkovic, C. Sialm, and S. Weisbenner. Portfolio concentration and the performance of individual investors. *Journal of Financial and Quantitative Analysis*, 43:613–656, 2008.

P. Jain. *Buffett Beyond Value: Why Warren Buffett Looks to Growth and Management When Investing*. Wiley and Sons, Hoboken, NJ, 2010.

N. Jegadeesh and S. Titman. Returns to buying winners and selling losers: Implications for stock market efficiency. *Journal of Finance*, 48:65–91, 1993.

M. Jensen. Some anomalous evidence regarding market efficiency. *Journal of Financial Economics*, 6:95–101, 1978.

G. Jiang, C. Lee, and Y. Zhang. Information uncertainty and expected returns. *Review of Accounting Studies*, 10:185–221, 2005.

C. M. Jones and O. Lamont. Short-sale constraints and stock returns. *Journal of Financial Economics*, 66:207–239, 2002.

D. Kahneman. *Attention and Effort*. Prentice-Hall, Englewood Cliffs, NJ, 1973.

D. Kahneman and A. Tversky. Judgment under uncertainty: Heuristics and biases. *Science*, 185:1124–1131, 1974.

M. Kamstra, L. Kramer, and M. Levi. Losing sleep at the market: The daylight saving anomaly. *American Economic Review*, 12:1000–1005, 2000.

M. Kamstra, L. Kramer, and M. Levi. Losing sleep at the market: The daylight saving anomaly: Reply. *American Economic Review*, 92:1257–1263, 2002.

M. Kamstra, L. Kramer, and M. Levi. Winter blues: A SAD stock market cycle. *American Economic Review*, 93:324–343, 2003.

M. Kamstra, L. Kramer, M. Levi, and R. Wermers. Seasonal asset allocation: Evidence from mutual fund flows. Working paper, York University, University of Toronto, University of British Columbia, and University of Maryland, 2013.

M. Kamstra, L. Kramer, M. Levi, and T. Wang. Seasonally varying preferences: Theoretical foundations for an empirical regularity. *Review of Asset Pricing Studies*, 4:39–77, 2014.

D. Keim and A. Madhavan. Transaction costs and investment style: An inter-exchange analysis of institutional equity trades. *Journal of Financial Economics*, 46:265–292, 1997.

J. Keynes. *The General Theory of Employment, Interest, and Money*. Harcourt Brace Jovanovich, New York, 1936.

M. Khan, L. Kogan, and G. Serafeim. Mutual fund trading pressure: Firm-level stock price impact and timing of SEOs. *Journal of Finance*, 67:1371–1395, 2012.

A. Kleidon. Variance bounds tests and stock price valuation models. *Journal of Political Economy*, 94:953–1001, 1986.

A. Kleidon. The probability of gross violations of a present value variance inequity: Reply. *Journal of Political Economy*, 96:1093–1096, 1988.

J. Kolari and S. Pynnönen. Event study testing with cross-sectional correlation of abnormal returns. *Review of Financial Studies*, 23:3996–4025, 2010.

A. Kolasinski, A. Reed, and O. Riggenberg. A multiple lender approach to understanding search and supply in the equity lending market. *Journal of Finance*, 68:559–595, 2013.

S. P. Kothari. Capital market research in accounting. *Journal of Accounting and Economics*, 31:105–231, 2001.

S. P. Kothari and J. A. Shanken. Book-to-market, dividend yield, and expected market returns: A time-series analysis. *Journal of Financial Economics*, 44:169–203, 1997.

S. P. Kothari and J. B. Warner. Measuring long-horizon security price performance. *Journal of Financial Economics*, 43:301–339, 1997.

A. Kumar. Who gambles in the stock market? *Journal of Finance*, 64:1889–1933, 2009.

A. Kumar and C. Lee. Retail investor sentiment and return comovements. *Journal of Finance*, 61:2451–2486, 2006.

A. Kyle. Continuous auctions and insider trading. *Econometrica*, 53:1315–1335, 1985.

R. La Porta. Expectations and the cross-section of stock returns. *Journal of Finance*, 51:1715–1742, 1996.

J. Lakonishok, A. Shleifer, and R. Vishny. Contrarian investment, extrapolation, and risk. *Journal of Finance*, 49:1541–1578, 1994.

O. Lamont. Investment plans and stock returns. *Journal of Finance*, 55:2719–2745, 2000.

M. Lang and R. Lundholm. The relation between security returns, firm earnings, and industry earnings. *Contemporary Accounting Research*, 13:607–629, 1996.

D. Larcker, E. So, and C. Wang. Boardroom centrality and firm performance. *Journal of Accounting and Economics*, 55:225–250, 2013.

C. Lee. Accounting-based valuation: A commentary. *Accounting Horizons*, 13:413–425, 1999.

C. Lee. Market efficiency and accounting research. *Journal of Accounting and Economics*, 31:233–253, 2001.

C. Lee and B. Swaminathan. Price momentum and trading volume. *Journal of Finance*, 55:2017–2070, 2000.

C. Lee, A. Shleifer, and R. Thaler. Investor sentiment and the closed-end fund puzzle. *Journal of Finance*, 46:75–109, 1991.

C. Lee, J. Myers, and B. Swaminathan. What is the intrinsic value of the Dow? *Journal of Finance*, 54:1693–1741, 1999.

R. Lehavy and R. Sloan. Investor recognition and stock returns. *Review of Accounting Studies*, 13:327–361, 2008.

B. Lehman. Earnings, dividend policy, and present value relations: Building blocks of dividend policy invariant cash flows. *Review of Quantitative Finance and Accounting*, 3:263–282, 1993.

M. Lemmon and E. Portniaguina. Consumer confidence and asset prices: Some empirical evidence. *Review of Financial Studies*, 19:1499–1529, 2006.

S. LeRoy and R. Porter. The present value relation: Tests based on implied variance bounds. *Econometrica*, 49:555–574, 1981.

D. Lesmond, J. Ogden, and C. Trzcinka. A new estimate of transaction costs. *Review of Financial Studies*, 12:1113–1141, 1999.

M. Lettau and J. Wachter. Why is long-horizon equity less risky? A duration-based explanation of the value premium. *Journal of Finance*, 62:55–92, 2007.

B. Lev. On the usefulness of earnings and earnings research: Lessons and directions from two decades of empirical research. *Journal of Accounting Research*, 27:153–192, 1989.

R. Libby, R. Bloomfield, and M. Nelson. Experimental research in financial accounting. *Accounting, Organizations and Society*, 27:775–810, 2002.

S. Lim and S. Teoh. Limited attention. In *Behavioral Finance: Investors, Corporations, and Markets*. Wiley Publishers, 2010.

J. Liu and J. Thomas. Stock returns and accounting earnings. *Journal of Accounting Research*, 38:71–101, 2000.

A. Ljungqvist and W. Qian. How constraining are limits to arbitrage? Working paper, NYU and Singapore NUS Business School, 2014.

D. Lou. A flow-based explanation for return predictability. *Review of Financial Studies*, 25:3457–3489, 2012.

D. Lou, H. Yan, and J. Zhang. Anticipated and repeated shocks in liquid markets. *Review of Financial Studies*, 26:1890–1912, 2013.

T. Loughran and J. Ritter. The new issues puzzle. *Journal of Finance*, 50: 23–51, 1995.

T. Loughran, J. Ritter, and K. Rydqvist. Initial public offerings: International insights. *Pacific-Basin Finance Journal*, 2:165–199, 1994.

R. Lundholm. A tutorial on the Ohlson and Feltham/Ohlson models: Answers to some frequently-asked questions. *Contemporary Accounting Research*, 11: 749–762, 1995.

E. Lyandres, L. Sun, and L. Zhang. The new issues puzzle: Testing the investment-based explanation. *Review of Financial Studies*, 21:2825–2855, 2008.

A. Madhavan and A. Sobczyk. Price dynamics and liquidity of exchange-traded funds. Working paper, Blackrock Inc., 2014.

B. Malkiel and E. Fama. Efficient capital markets: A review of theory and empirical work. *Journal of Finance*, 25:383–417, 1970.

S. Malpezzi. A simple error correction model of house prices. *Journal of Housing Economics*, 8:27–26, 1999.

T. Marsh and R. Merton. Dividend variability and variance bound tests for the rationality of stock market prices. *American Economic Review*, 76: 483–498, 1986.

C. Mashruwala, S. Rajgopal, and T. Shevlin. Why is the accrual anomaly not arbitraged away? The role of idiosyncratic risk and transaction costs. *Journal of Accounting and Economics*, 42:3–33, 2006.

D. McLean, J. Pontiff, and A. Watanabe. Share issuance and cross-sectional returns: International evidence. *Journal of Financial Economics*, 94:1–17, 2009.

R. McLean and J. Pontiff. Does academic research destroy stock return predictability? Working Paper, University of Alberta and MIT, 2013.

R. Mendenhall. Arbitrage risk and post-earnings-announcement drift. *Journal of Business*, 77:875–894, 2004.

L. Menzly and O. Ozbas. Market segmentation and cross-predictability of returns. *Journal of Finance*, 65:1555–1580, 2010.

R. Merton. A simple model of capital market equilibrium with incomplete information. *Journal of Finance*, 42:483–510, 1987.

J. Michels. Disclosure versus recognition: Inferences from subsequent events. Working paper, University of Pennsylvania, 2013.

S. Miller. Monetary dynamics: An application of cointegration and error-correction modeling. *Journal of Money, Credit and Banking*, pages 139–154, 1991.

M. Mitchell, T. Pulvino, and E. Stafford. Limited arbitrage in equity markets. *Journal of Finance*, 57:551–584, 2002.

P. Mohanram. Separating winners from losers among low book-to-market stocks using financial statement analysis. *Review of Accounting Studies*, 10:133–170, 2005.

M. Muller, E. Riedl, and T. Sellhorn. Recognition versus disclosure of fair values. *The Accounting Review*, 2015. Forthcoming.

W. Nelson. The aggregate change in shares and the level of stock prices. Working paper, Federal Reserve Board, 1999.

J. Ng, T. Rusticus, and R. Verdi. Implications of transaction costs for the post-earnings announcement drift. *Journal of Accounting Research*, 46: 661–696, 2008.

R. Novy-Marx. The other side of value: The gross profitability premium. *Journal of Financial Economics*, 108:1–28, 2013.

R. Novy-Marx. Predicting anomaly performance with politics, the weather, global warming, sunspots, and the stars. *Journal of Financial Economics*, 112(2):137–146, 2014.

K. Nyborg and P. Ostberg. Money and liquidity in financial markets. *Journal of Financial Economics*, 112:30–52, 2014.

J. Ohlson. Financial ratios and the probabilistic prediction of bankruptcy. *Journal of Accounting Research*, 18:109–131, 1980.

J. Ohlson. A synthesis of security valuation theory and the role of dividends, cash flows, and earnings. *Contemporary Accounting Research*, 6:648–676, 1990.

J. Ohlson. The theory of value and earnings, and an introduction to the Ball-Brown analysis. *Contemporary Accounting Research*, 7:1–19, 1991.

J. Ohlson. Earnings, book values, and dividends in security valuation. *Contemporary Accounting Research*, 11:661–687, 1995.

J. Ohlson. On successful research. *European Accounting Review*, 20(1), 2011.

J. Ohlson and P. Bilinski. Risk vs. anomaly: A new methodology applied to accruals. *The Accounting Review*, 2015. Forthcoming.

J. Ohlson and B. Juettner-Nauroth. Expected EPS and EPS growth as determinants of value. *Review of Accounting Studies*, 10:349–365, 2005.

J. O'Shaughnessy. *What Works on Wall Street,* 4th Edition. McGraw-Hill, 2011.

J. Ou and S. Penman. Financial statement analysis and the prediction of stock returns. *Journal of Accounting and Economics*, 11:295–329, 1989.

L. Pastor and R. Stambaugh. Costs of equity capital and model mispricing. *Journal of Finance*, 54:67–121, 1999.

K. Peasnell. Some formal connections between economic values and yields and accounting numbers. *Journal of Business Finance and Accounting*, 9: 361–381, 1982.

L. Pedersen. *Efficiently Inefficient.* Princeton University Press, Princeton, NJ, 2015.

L. Peng and W. Xiong. Investor attention, overconfidence and category learning. *Journal of Financial Economics*, 80:563–602, 2006.

S. Penman. An evaluation of accounting rate-of-return. *Journal of Accounting, Auditing, and Finance*, 6:233–255, 1991.

S. Penman. The articulation of price-earnings ratios and market-to-book ratios and the evaluation of growth. *Journal of Accounting Research*, 34: 235–259, 1996.

S. Penman. A synthesis of equity valuation techniques and the terminal value calculation for the dividend discount model. *Review of Accounting Studies*, 2:303–323, 1997.

S. Penman. *Accounting for Value*. Columbia University Press, 2010.

S. Penman. *Financial Statement Analysis and Security Valuation,* 5th Edition. McGraw-Hill/Irwin, 2012.

S. Penman, S. Richardson, and I. Tuna. The book-to-price effect in stock returns: Accounting for leverage. *Journal of Accounting Research*, 45:427–467, 2007.

S. Penman, F. Reggiani, S. Richardson, and I. Tuna. An accounting-based characteristic model for asset pricing. Working paper, Columbia University, Bocconi University, and London Business School, 2014.

R. Petkova and L. Zhang. Is value riskier than growth? *Journal of Financial Economics*, 78:187–202, 2005.

U. Peyer and T. Vermaelen. The nature and persistence of buyback anomalies. *Review of Financial Studies*, 22:1693–1745, 2009.

M. Pinegar. Losing sleep at the market: Comment. *American Economic Review*, 92:1251–1256, 2002.

J. Piotroski. Value investing: The use of historical financial statement information to separate winners from losers. *Journal of Accounting Research*, 38:1–41, 2000.

J. Piotroski and E. So. Identifying expectation errors in value/glamour strategies: A fundamental analysis approach. *Review of Financial Studies*, 25: 2841–2875, 2012.

J. Pontiff. Costly arbitrage: Evidence from closed-end funds. *Quarterly Journal of Economics*, 111:1135–1152, 1996.

J. Pontiff and W. Woodgate. Share issuance and cross-sectional returns. *Journal of Finance*, 63:921–945, 2008.

G. Preinreich. Annual survey of economic theory: The theory of depreciation. *Econometrica*, 6:219–241, 1938.

A. Puckett and X. Yan. Short-term institutional herding and its impact on stock prices. Working paper, University of Missour, 2013.

A. K. Purnanandam and B. Swaminathan. Are ipos really underpriced? *Review of Financial Studies*, 17:811–848, 2004.

E. Qian, R. Hua, and E. Sorensen. *Quantitative Equity Portfolio Management: Modern Techniques and Applications.* Chapman and Hall, 2007.

M. Reinganum. Misspecification of capital asset pricing: Empirical anomalies based on earnings' yield and market values. *Journal of Financial Economics*, 9:19–46, 1981.

S. Richardson, R. Sloan, M. Soliman, and I. Tuna. Accrual reliability, earnings persistence, and stock prices. *Journal of Accounting and Economics*, 39: 437–485, 2005.

S. Richardson, I. Tuna, and P. Wysocki. Accounting anomalies and fundamental analysis: A review of recent research advances. *Journal of Accounting and Economics*, 50:410–454, 2010.

S. Richardson, R. Sloan, and H. You. What makes stock prices move? Fundamentals vs investor recognition. *Financial Analysts Journal*, 68:30–50, 2012.

J. Ritter. The long-run performance of initial public offerings. *Journal of Finance*, 46:3–27, 1991.

R. Roll. Orange juice and weather. *American Economic Review*, 74:861–880, 1984.

R. Roll. R-squared. *Journal of Finance*, 43:541–566, 1988.

B. Rosenberg, K. Reid, and R. Lanstein. Persuasive evidence of market inefficiency. *Journal of Portfolio Management*, 11:9–17, 1985.

M. Rubinstein. Rational markets: Yes or no? The affirmative case. *Financial Analysts Journal*, 5:15–29, 2001.

R. Sadka. Momentum and post-earnings-announcement drift anomalies: The role of liquidity risk. *Journal of Financial Economics*, 80:309–349, 2006.

T. Santos and P. Veronesi. Habit-formation, the cross-section of stock returns and the cash-flow risk puzzle. *Journal of Financial Economics*, 98:385–413, 2010.

E. Saunders. Stock prices and wall street weather. *American Economic Review*, 83:1337–1345, 1993.

K. Schipper. Required disclosure in financial reports. *The Accounting Review*, 82:301–326, 2007.

N. Schwarz, F. Strack, D. Kommer, and D. Wagner. Soccer, rooms, and the quality of your life: Mood effects on judgements of satisfaction with life in general and with specific domains. *European Journal of Social Psychology*, 17:69–79, 1987.

K. Schweitzer, D. Zillman, J. Weaver, and E. Luttrell. Perception of threatening events in the emotional aftermath of a televised college football game. *Journal of Broadcasting and Electronic Media*, 26:75–82, 1992.

W. Sharpe and G. Alexander. *Investments*, 4th Edition. Prentice Hall, Englewood Cliffs, NJ, 1990.

R. Shiller. The volatility of long-term interest rates and expectation models of the term structure. *Journal of Political Economy*, 87:1190–1219, 1979.

R. Shiller. The use of volatility measures in assessing market efficiency. *Journal of Finance*, 36:291–304, 1981a.

R. Shiller. Do stock prices move too much to be justified by subsequent changes in dividends? *American Economic Review*, 71:421–436, 1981b.

R. Shiller. Stock prices and social dynamics. *The Brookings Papers on Economic Activity*, 2:457–510, 1984.

R. Shiller. The probability of gross violations of a present value variance inequality. *Journal of Political Economy*, 96:1089–1092, 1988.

R. Shiller. Human behavior and the efficiency of the financial system. In J. B. Taylor and M. Woodford, editors, *Handbook of Macroeconomics*, volume 1, pages 1305–40, 1999.

R. Shiller. *Irrational Exuberance*. Princeton University Press, Princeton, NJ, 2000.

S. Shive and H. Yun. Are mutual funds sitting ducks? *Journal of Financial Economics*, 107:220–237, 2013.

A. Shleifer. Do demand curves for stocks slope down? *Journal of Finance*, 41:579–590, 1986.

A. Shleifer. *Inefficient Markets: An Introduction to Behavioral Finance*. Oxford University Press, Oxford, UK, 2000.

A. Shleifer and L. Summers. The noise trader approach to finance. *Journal of Economic Perspectives*, 34:19–33, 1990.

A. Shleifer and R. Vishny. The limits of arbitrage. *Journal of Finance*, 52: 35–55, 1997.

A. Shleifer and R. Vishny. Fire sales in finance and macroeconomics. *Journal of Economic Perspectives*, 25:29–48, 2011.

G. Shub, B. Beardsley, H. Donnadieu, K. Kramer, A. Maguire, P. Morel, and T. Tang. Global asset management 2013: Capitalizing on the Recovery. Boston Consulting Group, 2013.

T. Shumway. The delisting bias in CRSP data. *Journal of Finance*, 52:327–340, 1997.

C. Sims. Implications of rational inattention. *Journal of Monetary Economics*, 50:665–690, 2003.

E. Sirri and P. Tufano. Costly search and mutual fund flows. *Journal of Finance*, 53:1589–1622, 1998.

R. Sloan. Do stock prices fully reflect information in accruals and cash flows about future earnings? *The Accounting Review*, 71:289–316, 1996.

E. So. A new approach to predicting analyst forecast errors: Do investors overweight analyst forecasts? *Journal of Financial Economics*, 108:615–640, 2013.

E. So and S. Wang. News-driven return reversals: Liquidity provision ahead of earnings announcements. *Journal of Financial Economics*, 2014. Forthcoming.

K. Spiess and J. Affleck-Graves. Underperformance in long-run stock returns following seasoned equity offerings. *Journal of Financial Economics*, 38: 243–267, 1995.

K. Spiess and J. Affleck-Graves. The long-run performance of stock returns after debt offerings. *Journal of Financial Economics*, 54:45–73, 1999.

D. Stattman. Book values and stock returns. *The Chicago MBA: A Journal of Selected Papers*, 4:25–45, 1980.

J. Stein. Rational capital budgeting in an irrational world. *Journal of Business*, 69:429–55, 1996.

J. Stein. Presidential address: Sophisticated investors and market efficiency. *Journal of Finance*, 64:1517–1548, 2009.

S. H. Teoh and T. J. Wong. Why new issues and high-accrual firms underperform: The role of analysts' credulity. *Review of Financial Studies*, 15 (3):869–900, 2002.

R. Thaler. The end of behavioral finance. *Financial Analysts Journal*, 55: 12–17, 1999.

J. Tobin. On the efficiency of the financial system. *Lloyds Bank Review*, 153: 1–15, 1984.

M. Vassalou. News related to future gdp growth as a risk factor in equity returns. *Journal of Financial Economics*, 68:47–73, 2003.

T. Vuolteenaho. What drives firm-level stock returns? *Journal of Finance*, 57:233–264, 2002.

J. Wahlen, S. Baginski, and M. Bradshaw. *Financial Reporting, Financial Statement Analysis and Valuation: A Strategic Perspective,* 7th Edition. Cengage Learning, 2010.

D. Wann, M. Melnick, G. Russell, and D. Pease. Relationships between spectator identification and spectators' perceptions of influence, spectators' emotions, and competition outcome. *Journal of Sport and Exercise Psychology*, 16:347–364, 1994.

K. West. Dividend innovations and stock price volatility. *Econometrica*, 56: 37–61, 1988.

K. Yu. Does recognition versus disclosure affect value relevance? Evidence from pension accounting. *The Accounting Review*, 88:1095–1127, 2013.

K. Yuan, L. Zheng, and Q. Zhu. Are investors moonstruck? Lunar phases and stock returns. *Journal of Empirical Finance*, 13:1–23, 2006.

L. Zacks. *The Handbook of Equity Market Anomalies: Translating Market Inefficiencies into Effective Investment Strategies*. Wiley and Sons, 2011.

F. Zhang. Information uncertainty and stock returns. *Journal of Finance*, 61: 105–137, 2006a.

F. Zhang. Information uncertainty and analyst forecast behavior. *Contemporary Accounting Research*, 23:565–590, 2006b.

L. Zhang. The value premium. *Journal of Finance*, 60:67–103, 2005.

X. Zhang. Conservative accounting and equity valuation. *Journal of Accounting and Economics*, 29:125–149, 2000.

X. Zhou and S. Jain. *Active Equity Management*. Self-published, 2014.

CPSIA information can be obtained
at www.ICGtesting.com
Printed in the USA
FSOW03n1719030216
16486FS

9 781601 988928